WC

INTRODUCTION

I n the days of the British Empire, the Seven Years' War was a landmark in schools' history lessons. The 'year of miracles', 1759, when Horace Walpole could write only half mockingly 'one can never afford to miss a single copy of a newspaper for fear of missing a British victory somewhere', was still a matter not only of pride, but also of great interest. Only in America, despite the matchless splendour of Francis Parkman's writing on the period, was the 'French and Indian War', as the Seven Years' War has always been called there, rather neglected. It was a 'colonial days' campaign in the minds of later Americans for whom life began in the 1770s, and only in states where the battles had been fought was it – and is it – much recalled.

Today, the neglect spans the Atlantic with only one exception: the story of Wolfe at Quebec is still a matter of passionate interest far outside Canada. Canadians feel its effects to this day, and Americans have cause to remember it, for in winning the battle, the British, as we shall see, lost America. The fascination with Wolfe and his army is understandable, and a considerable part of this book is devoted to the campaign; but it was only part of an extraordinary story, for, even by British standards, the French and Indian War was a classic example of early bungling which bravery could not counterbalance, followed by inspired leadership of that much abused but magnificent figure, the British redcoat. Many provincials, too, contributed to the victory despite inter-colony bickering and jealousies, and natural resentment of the arrogance of too many British officers and officials. They learned lessons which were soon to rebound on the mother country. The cast list of this ferocious, often terrifying war, much of it fought in forests which must have seemed to the redcoats to be a wilderness of tigers, is an impressive one: the young Washington; Sir William Johnson, the land-hungry empire-builder who was genuinely liked and trusted by Indians; Lord Howe, the incomparable young officer whose death at Ticonderoga was nothing less than a national tragedy; the unfortunate Braddock; Rogers and his Rangers; the malicious Townshend; the appalling Abercromby; and, above all, the heroic twin heroes of the great drama, Montcalm and Wolfe. And always there was the

CANADA

QUEBEC
MONTREAL
Ft. FRONTENAC
OSWEGO   Ft.TICONDEROGA
NIAGARA   Ft.WILLIAM HENRY   Ft.EDWARD BOSTON
ALBANY
NEW YORK
VENANGO
DUQUESNE   BEDFORD   PHILADELPHIA
Ft.NECESSITY   CUMBERLAND
BALTIMORE
ALEXANDRIA

WILLIAMSBURG

3

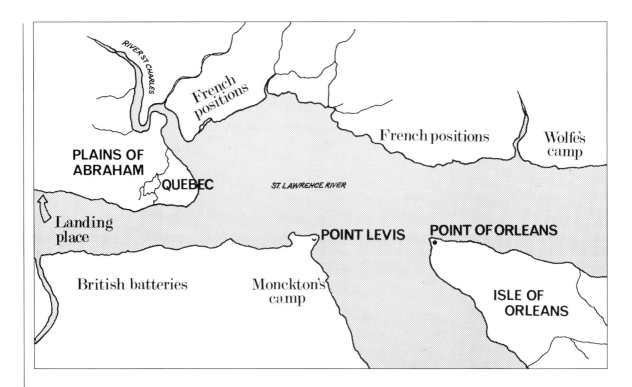

redcoat, the central figure of this book. The body of the text is a history of the war from a military point of view; the colour plates and their captions are mainly devoted to the uniforms of the redcoats, their leaders, and their allies. No one who has studied the redcoat fails to respond to his cheerfulness, his own response to good leadership, his bravery when things (as so often) went wrong, his occasional disgraceful behaviour in battle, his sheer guts. The concept of empire can rightly be criticised, even attacked, and apologists must recognise its faults as well as its many virtues. But those who attack the redcoats, those who cannot respond to their valour and, indeed, the valour of their enemies, are to be pitied.

THE UNENDING CONFLICT

'A volley from the hunting-pieces of a few backwoodsmen, commanded by a Virginian youth, George Washington', is how Francis Parkman described the obscure action in 1754 which precipitated the French and Indian War and, in Horace Walpole's phrase, 'set the world on fire'. The 'Father of his Country' began making history when he was a 22-year-old acting lieutenant-colonel of militia.

So began the struggle that Winston Churchill called 'the first world war'. Yet in North America there had been little peace during the 18th century. The war was part of the seemingly unending conflict between France and England to decide the fate of a continent.

There had already been two official Anglo-French wars, the second of which ended in 1748. The treaty-makers returned to each country the conquests of the other. The commercially hopeful town of Madras to Britain, and Louisbourg to France, much to the legitimate fury of the

Although no Foot Guards served in America at this time, this picture merits inclusion as the best of Morier's grenadier paintings, illustrating clearly the cut of the uniforms and several small details of interest. The uniforms of all infantry were basically the same, distinguished for grenadiers by mitre caps and shoulder-wings – see description of colour plates A1, A2 and A3 for general information. Lapels could be buttoned across in foul weather, or half-buttoned for marching. Belts were light-coloured buff leather; a heavy one over the right shoulder supported the polished black cartridge-box. Grenadiers no longer carried grenades at this time; they were the élite company of each regiment. Grenadier status was indicated by a perforated, stoppered brass tube above the brass buckle, originally the match-case.

A tightly coiled match may have been worn on the belt behind the shoulder. The waistbelt supported the sword-'hanger' and bayonet in a double frog; usually only grenadiers carried the hanger in the field. A picker and brush for clearing the touch-hole of the musket hang by fine chains from the end of the shoulder-belt. Note the visible front breeches buttons – unfashionable, but still usual among common soldiers. White gaiters with 36 black buttons are worn for formal duty, replaced by black, brown or grey ones for 'marching and common duties'. Muskets had steel or wooden ramrods – sometimes both within the same unit. The small figure in the left background, and the right-hand grenadier, wear corporals' shoulder-knots on the right shoulder. (Reproduced by gracious permission of H.M. the Queen)

New Englanders who had captured the great fortress on Cape Breton Island with naval aid in 1745.

The 'peace' that followed in America was no peace at all. The vastly outnumbered French – there were about 55,000 of them in contrast to about a million and a half English colonists — were the leading power in North America, even though their position was built on sand. Most

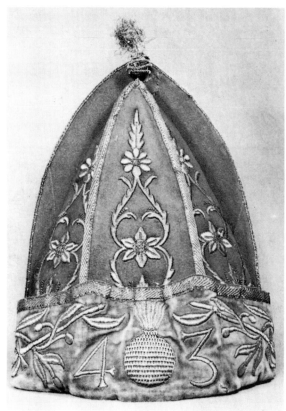

Front and back views of a fine example of a grenadier officer's mitre cap of the 43rd Foot, with elaborate embroidery in coloured silks, silver and gold. Officers' caps may have sometimes varied in details of design and quality within a regiment, depending on the taste and purse of the individual officer. (National Army Museum)

Indians preferred the French Canadians, who had little of the racial prejudice of the Anglo-Americans; they were traders, explorers, adventurers and, except along the St Lawrence, not settlers. Only the Five Nations of the Iroquois Confederacy (Six Nations since 1715 when the Tuscaroras were allowed to join the Mohawks, Oneidas, Onondagas, Cayugas and Senecas) tended to side with the British or remain neutral. No longer the power they once were, these proud, fierce advanced tribes lived in what is now central New York State, but lorded it over a much wider area. Fortunately a trader and agent, William Johnson, later to be Sir William and the greatest landowner in North America, had enormous influence over them, and especially over the Mohawks. He liked the men and loved the women: his last wife (in all but name) was the lovely Molly Brant, sister of the great Joseph Brant, the Mohawk war chief for whom an extraordinary career in war and peace lay in the future. By 1748 the fur trade had led too many Indians to become dependent on white goods, everything from trinkets to armaments, which the English could supply more easily than the French. Loyalty to New France was strained, but two factors played into French hands. Though Quebec, their capital, was priest-ridden and though the fur trade was rotten with corruption, the French Canadians were better soldiers than their rivals, having learnt the art of woodland fighting with their Indian allies; and, more significantly, for all their lack of unity, the English colonists, as we have seen, wanted land.

No Indians ever really understood this lust for land. To Indians, the earth was sacred, a mother, not something to be bartered or owned. It

could be hunted over, fought over or even farmed – by the women – but owned in the white sense, never!

Indian warfare against the whites was total. Terror was an instrument of policy. The whites brought warfare on themselves by repeated betrayals or misunderstandings, and vengeance bred vengeance until savagery was rampant on both sides. The redcoats were to find themselves in a nightmare world where the disciplines of Europe had no counterpart (until the Quebec campaign, which was not so very different from the European style of warfare).

In 1747, the Ohio Land Company was formed to open up the fertile lands of the Ohio Valley. In 1749 the company got its first land grant of 200,000 acres on both sides of the Ohio and sent its first scouts across the mountains the next year. Soon, English colonists who were killed were likely to have dirt stuffed into their mouths, for the Indians knew what the Ohio Company and the independent prospectors were after.

Meanwhile, in 1749, a French and Indian party swept down into the Ohio Valley to claim it for France, optimistically putting notices on trees and burying engraved plates to enforce their claim. The Ohio Company established a base at Wills Creek, now Cumberland, Maryland. Trails were blazed westwards to the Monongahela River to find suitable land for settlement. With French influence among the Indians spreading fast, the stage was set for an encounter to decide who would rule the Forks of the Ohio, the Monongahela and the Allegheny – and the whole valley.

In 1753, the new Governor of Canada, Marquis Duquesne, sent 4,000 men south to build forts. Fort Presqu'île was erected on Lake Erie and

Front and back views of a typical other ranks' mitre cap, in this case of the 49th Foot, though all followed more or less the same pattern. The regimental facing colour appeared on the front and on the band at the base of the back. The back and the small front flap with the white horse of Hanover were of red cloth. The GR cipher, usually flanked by decorative scrollwork, was in various colours, the crown in full colour. The cap was bound with white tape, and surmounted by a tuft in regimental colours, missing here. The horse usually rode over a strip of 'ground' in green and yellow. The band at the back was embroidered in a variety of ways, often with a grenade, the regimental number, and scrolls. Certain units with Royal or Ancient badges carried them in full colours in place of the cipher. (National Army Museum)

Morier painting of grenadiers in marching order. These three regiments all served in America: the 46th Foot from 1758 to 1767, the 47th and 48th from 1758 to 1763. Colonel Thomas Murray's 46th served at Ticonderoga in 1758. Facings are yellow, lace white with red and yellow stripes and a double dark blue zigzag. Note the pigtail tucked up under the cap, and the white stock buckled at the rear. Colonel Peregrine Lascelles' 47th had white facings, and the white lace bore two black zigzags with a row of black dots in between. Colonel Daniel Webb's 48th wore distinctions as in colour plate B4; the scrollwork on the cap is white, the cipher green. For marching order drab-coloured gaiters would actually have been worn. Cowhide knapsacks and tin canteens are slung on the left, and a haversack of greyish canvas on the right, over the cartridge-box. It is possible that painted canvas covers protected the caps. Sections of the six-man tents, tent poles and camp kettles would be divided among the men on the march. Waistbelts were often worn over the right shoulder, the bayonet and – for grenadiers – the sword hanging under the left arm. An extra cartridge-box was often worn on a buff or black strap buckled over the waistbelt. Note the centre man's open collar and lack of stock. (Reproduced by gracious permission of H.M. the Queen)

Fort le Boeuf below it. The English post at Venango was taken, and garrisons left at each of them.

The alarmed Governor of Virginia, Robert Dinwiddie, sent a warning to Legardeur de St Pierre, who was in command at Fort le Boeuf since the previous commander had died of dysentery, informing him that he was trespassing on Virginian soil. Not surprisingly, St Pierre disagreed, so Dinwiddie sent Major George Washington, 21 years old, over six feet tall and eager for land and a regular commission, to see him. His small escort of frontiersmen was joined on the way by a friendly Seneca, Half King, and some of his band. St Pierre politely received Washington, refused to budge, and, without success, tried to seduce the Senecas, known, confusingly, in that area as Mingoes. Washington returned and reported to the governor, urging that a fort should be built at the Forks of the Ohio.

After a struggle, Dinwiddie got a little money out of his assembly, and, in April 1754, work on the fort began. Suddenly, 500 Frenchmen materialised out of the forest and the British surrendered and were sent home. The victors proceeded to erect Fort Duquesne, a famous spot, later to be Fort Pitt and, finally, Pittsburg.

This was war, or so the Virginians thought, even though neighbouring colonies showed typical lack of interest. Washington, now an acting lieutenant-colonel and 22, was put in charge of a 300-strong party and was met at Great Meadows by Half King, who told him that some French and Indians were near by. On 28 May the Americans took the French by surprise, wounded a few men, killed their leader de Jumonville and took 21 prisoners. The war, undeclared for another two years, had started.

Washington learned that 500 Frenchmen were on their way to meet de Jumonville and retreated to Great Meadows, where he was joined by men from two Independent Companies, commanded by Captain McKay, a regular, who outranked Colonel Washington, a mere volunteer. This situation was all too common throughout the ensuing war and naturally upset the young Virginian. Washington still hoped to push on to Duquesne, but, hearing that the French were now near, he and his exhausted, starving men retreated again to Great Meadows and built Fort Necessity, dangerously far from water and exposed to fire from wooded slopes.

The fire came on the night of 2 July, directed by de Jumonville's brother, Coulon de Villiers. In heavy rain, the British fought bravely for nine hours, refused a surrender call, but finally, when a quarter of the ragged, sick garrison of some 400 had been killed or wounded, they gave in. It was a cruel blow to the ambitious young Washington. However, the British marched out with the honours of war, leaving swivel guns and military baggage behind. Two significant things occurred. An interpreter botched his job and made Washington unwittingly sign that he was the assassin of de Jumonville, an excellent propaganda weapon for the French; and a Scotsman named Robert Stobo was chosen as one of the hostages to be left. He later rendered great services, first at Fort Duquesne, then at Quebec. But the immediate effect of the defeat was sheer disaster. The Indians rightly believed the French to be the masters of the situation, while de Villiers returned to Fort Duquesne having seen to it, as Parkman put it, that 'Not an English flag now waved beyond the Alleghenies'.

Rare contemporary illustrations of Indians: the war chieftain with scalp in hand, and the Ottawa warrior with his family, were sketched by George Townshend. (Courtauld Institute of Art)

The 'French Castle' at Old Fort Niagara, a massive stone fortified building erected by the French in 1726. (Old Fort Niagara Assoc. Inc.)

DISASTER

When the news of Washington's humiliation reached Europe, British and French officials in Paris were still arguing about the previous war. France's numerical weakness in North America in 1754 was more than offset by the total unreadiness of the British to fight a major war on any front. Not that anything as foolhardy as a declaration of war was made. Instead, and despite the inadequacies of the incompetent Prime Minister, the Duke of Newcastle, an attempt was made to improve the armed services. It was high time. The navy had 200 over-extended ships, many of them in poor condition, and the army was down to less than 20,000 men. But in July 1754, before the news of Fort Necessity had reached Europe, money and arms were sent across the Atlantic, and in late September, when the worst was known, the 44th and the 48th Foot were ordered to sail from Cork to North America. Each battalion was about 350 strong with additional drafts of variable quality added to them, bringing them up to 500 each, and it was hoped that Americans would later be recruited.

In command was a 45-year-old Coldstreamer, Major-General Edward Braddock, a stern but by no means inhumane soldier who knew nothing of American conditions, but realised (as he told his actress friend, Anne Bellamy) that he would have to cut his way 'through unknown woods'. He said that he and his men were being sent like sacrifices to the altar.

Braddock reached Hampton Roads, Virginia, in February 1755. Meanwhile, 3,000 French regulars under Baron von Dieskau, who had served brilliantly under Marshal Saxe, were under orders for Canada. The provincials welcomed Braddock effusively. Now the redcoats could do their fighting for them! Braddock tactfully invited the touchy young Washington to serve as his aide-de-camp, which eased the Virginian's frustration at being outranked by the British regulars, but orders had come from London which confirmed that this offensive rule still applied. With few exceptions, British officers despised the provincials, and a dangerously mutual antipathy sprang up from the beginning.

It must be stressed, though, that the British had some reason to resent Americans in general. Pennsylvania refused to supply fighting troops for religious reasons, even though the most distant settlers of the Quaker colony badly needed protection. Braddock only got really adequate help from Virginia, and trying to get his expedition properly provisioned and fit for travel proved a nightmare. Local recruiting, however, got the 44th and 48th barely up to strength.

On 14 April, British officers and colonial governors agreed on a series of plans. First, the French must be cleared from the Forks of the Ohio and Fort Duquesne by Braddock. Meanwhile, the admirable Governor Shirley of Massachusetts was to head for Oswego, then attack Niagara, and William Johnson, now His Majesty's Commissioner of Indian Affairs, was to proceed up the Hudson and take Crown Point with New England volunteers and some of his fierce Iroquois friends. Finally, Brigadier Robert Monckton, was to deal with the French in Acadia with naval help.

Copyright© G.A. Embleton

Copyright© G.A. Embleton

TOP The cut of British infantry coats, based on careful examination of the paintings of David Morier and other sources. Morier's so-called '1751' paintings were commissioned by the Duke of Cumberland at about the time of new Royal Regulations controlling the army's uniforms. Recently a theoretical sequence and dates for these paintings have been presented as if established fact. Readers should remember that we do not know for certain when, and in what order, they were painted, nor how accurately they depict what was actually worn or what should have been worn. BOTTOM The coats and waistcoats worn by British light infantry, based on their regimentals with the lace removed and the laceless sleeves sewn on their regulation waistcoats (centre).

Interior of the guardroom at Old Fort Niagara, on the first floor. An interesting feature is the long undivided 'shelf' bunk, which held at least 30 men. (Old Fort Niagara Assoc. Inc.)

This bold plan, covering huge tracts of wilderness with split forces, was not so bad as subsequent events made it seem. Against the British, however, were some 3,000 French regulars, 15,000 militia, 2,000 colonial regulars of the Marine and an unknown number of Indians.

Braddock had one stroke of luck. The hostage taken at Fort Necessity, Robert Stobo, smuggled a plan of Fort Duquesne out to him. When his act was discovered, only the fact that the two nations were not yet officially at war saved him from execution, and instead he was sent to Quebec, where he was to be even more useful.

In May, Braddock reached the trading post of Wills Creek, making his headquarters at nearby Fort Cumberland. Let down by contractors and weakened by disease, the troops were badly delayed. They were in two brigades. Lieutenant-Colonel Sir Peter Halkett led his 44th Foot, now some 700 strong; there were 230 Rangers from Virginia, New York and Maryland, and 50 carpenters. Meanwhile Colonel Thomas Dunbar commanded the 48th, now 650 strong, 230 Rangers from Virginia and the Carolinas, and 35 carpenters. There were four 12-pdrs., six 6-pdrs, four 8-in. howitzers and 15 mortars. Both brigades also had one Independent Company from New York, while to help with the ferrying and block-and-tackle work, Lieutenant Charles Spendlowe from HMS *Norwich* was attached with a landing-party to the gunners.

Things at Wills Creek went from bad to worse. Braddock wanted 150 four-team wagons, plus wagoneers, and if it had not been for Benjamin Franklin, Postmaster of Pennsylvania, 'almost the only instance of ability and honesty I have known in the provinces', he would have got hardly any. As it was, 1,500 pack-horses were rounded up, many being promptly stolen by the locals, and wagons were found thanks to Franklin. Braddock resorted to fierce discipline to keep a grip on a deteriorating situation, but his many detractors rarely include Pennsylvanians, who regard what he achieved before the débâcle as remarkable.

This is partly because of the road which he and his men built on an Indian trail, which was surfaced and widened enough to take both guns and wagons. Often the most that could be marched was under four miles a day, and morale was not improved by short rations. At this time an ambush was unlikely, for scouts were out on the flanks and in front, while the axe-men hacked the road, which was to be more than 12 ft. wide. It was an amazing feat.

The expedition reached Little Meadows, the advance guard arriving on 25 June. Though stragglers had been picked off by French and Indian scouts, there was as yet no sign of a major French force. However, Braddock heard that 500 Frenchmen were marching to reinforce Fort Duquesne. At a council of war, Washington was asked for advice. Acting on it, Braddock decided to advance with 1,200 men, leaving Dunbar with the heavy baggage, the wagons and the womenfolk. An advance guard was to be led by Lieutenant-Colonel Thomas Gage, and it was this force that crossed the Monongahela on 9 July, eight miles from Fort Duquesne.

At the fort were about 1,000 French and Indians under Contrecœur. The new governor-general of Canada, the Marquis de Vaudreuil, could spare no more because of pressures elsewhere. Only on the 8th had the French heard that Braddock was approaching, and Contrecœur decided to ambush him at the Monongahela, choosing a party of 250 Frenchmen and 650 Indians under Captain Lienard de Beaujeu for the fight.

The British had been forced to ford the river twice to avoid a narrow defile and were engaged in a short skirmish at the second crossing with some 30 Indians who fled. Now they were in more open country, woods rather than thick forest. A band played and redcoats and provincials stepped out, with Braddock and his men following closely behind the advance guard in two columns. Grenadiers were on the flanks, Virginians in the rear, and cattle and pack-horses were between the columns. The sun shone on this army of the damned, its men jauntily confident that the French had already fled.

Waiting for them was Beaujeu, who had great difficulty in persuading his Indians to stay. Like them, he and his men were stripped for action and painted. Braddock's men marched on. Suddenly, Beaujeu appeared, turned and waved his hat to the men behind him. He was killed almost at once as the ambush site echoed to a terrifying war-cry, a blood-chilling moment for any Europeans hearing it for the first time. The redcoats swung from their columns into line as bullets tore into them from the trees. The French Canadians took to their heels, and only the prompt action of Captain Dumas and Charles Langlade, leading the Indians, prevented them from following the French. Yet despite this disarray in the enemy ranks, the British were doomed. They could not see their enemy, their whole training was foreign to the situation and, as the provincials sensibly took cover, the redcoats became so unnerved that they shot at them by mistake.

The officers on their horses were soon picked off by Indian marksmen, and their men went out of control. Braddock arrived with Washington; the former, who was nothing if not brave, did his best with curses and the flat of his sword to restore order, aided by the young Virginian. Five horses were shot under the general as the chaos became total. His men were broken up into heaving groups, totally without purpose, except for the Virginians. The few British who tried to take cover, Indian fashion, incurred their leader's wrath.

With 63 out of 86 of his officers killed or wounded, Braddock himself fell, shot through his arm and lung. He had just ordered a retreat, even though a panic-stricken flight

One of Brigadier Townshend's many waspish cartoons of Wolfe; though coarsely witty, they tended to demoralise his fellow staff officers, already disturbed by the long stalemate and their commander's illness. (McCord Museum)

The 1st or Royal Regiment of Foot, later the Royal Scots, wore red coats and waistcoats, blue breeches and facings, and plain white lace. The cap is blue, the crown is full colour, the green Order of the Thistle circlet bears the motto *Nemo Me Impune Lacessit*, and the cipher is yellow on blue; the red flap bears the usual white horse. Colonel James Sinclair's 2nd Battalion was at Ticonderoga in 1759, and remained in America until 1764. (Reproduced by gracious permission of H.M. the Queen)

Colonel Edward Whitmore's 22nd Foot served in America from 1758 to 1765. The facings were buff, the lace white with two red and blue stripes. The scrolls and cipher on the buff-fronted cap are yellow. (Reproduced by gracious permission of H.M. the Queen)

The 27th (Inniskilling) Foot served in America from 1758 to 1767; they were at Ticonderoga in 1758 and 1759. The facings were buff, the lace white with a yellow stripe between a blue and a black zigzag. The cap bears a blue roundel with a castle flying St George's flag beneath a scroll inscribed Inniskilling. (Reproduced by gracious permission of H.M. the Queen)

The 40th Foot, which seems to have gone through four colonels during its American service in 1758–65, wore buff facings; the lace had a black stripe edged each side with buff. The grenadier cap bears white scrollwork and a black cipher. (Reproduced by gracious permission of H.M. the Queen)

was already beginning. The Indians, as usual, were too busy with plunder to follow: the booty that they took included Braddock's chest containing all the British plans for the operations in the north and west.

Washington remained unwounded. It was he who brought the news of the disaster back to Dunbar, and he who later read the memorial service over Braddock's body when his chief died four days after the battle. He never ceased to admire the tough, brave Coldstreamer.

The British had suffered a catastrophe. Apart from the heavy loss of officers, over 914 NCOs and privates were killed or wounded out of a total of 1,300. The French lost only three officers killed and four wounded, and less than ten regulars and Canadians killed and wounded. Twenty-seven Indians were killed or wounded.

The fleeing redcoats met the supply wagons at Gist's Plantation, where they had been sent by Dunbar, but the panic went on. At Dunbar's

The 42nd Foot (The Highland Regiment), or more popularly The Black Watch, served in America from 1758 to 1767, and was famous for its part in the attack on Ticonderoga in 1758. Two battalions were in America in the winter of 1759–60. Coat and waistcoat were red, as was the flap embroidered with a white motif on the front of the fur grenadier cap. Collar and cuffs were buff; lace was white with two red stripes. Note that the collar is sewn to the coat below the strip of lace around the neck of the coat. Belts are black, the musket sling very dark buff. (Reproduced by gracious permission of H.M. the Queen)

Colonel James Kennedy's 43rd Foot served in America from 1758 to 1765. Facings were white, and the white lace had two red stripes with a row of black stars between. The cap has white scroll-work relieved in black, a dark blue cipher, and a blue and white tuft. Sir Peter Halkett's (later James Abercromby's) 44th Foot was one of the regiments involved in Braddock's Massacre, but served on in America until 1765. General colour details will be found in the description of colour plate B5. The grenadier corporal (centre) has white scrolls and a black cipher on his ochre-yellow cap front. The strip of lace on his right shoulder holds the knot of his rank, hanging down the back. Hugh Warburton's 45th Foot served in America from 1758 to 1765; its facings were a dark bluish green, its lace white with green stripes and stars. The mitre cap has white scrolls and cipher on its green front, and a green and white tuft. (Reproduced by gracious permission of H.M. the Queen)

camp, Dunbar himself ordered the destruction of everything: cannon, ammunition, powder wagons and shells, a disgraceful miscalculation even though another attack – wrongly – seemed imminent.

Braddock at least had learnt his lesson before he died. 'We shall know better how to deal with them another time,' he said, and he praised his Virginians, while whispering that he could not bear the sight of a redcoat. And, indeed, while the panic of the regulars was understandable, their reputation, and that of British soldiers in general, had taken a terrible beating. On 13 July, the retreat to Fort Cumberland began (Braddock's death occurred on the march). The triumph of the French and Indians was complete, though the victory had been almost entirely an Indian one. Back in England, a young officer named James Wolfe commented: 'Our military education is by far the worst in Europe', and significantly complained: 'All our concerns are treated with contempt or totally neglected.'

The inner fort at Fort Ligonier, built by Brigadier John Forbes on his march into the Ohio Valley in 1758: a reconstruction which follows the original plans. (S. Fredman)

The year 1755 was not a total disaster for British arms, however. Monckton, in command of the minor expedition against Acadia, led New Englanders and a few redcoats against Fort Beauséjour successfully. The fort, situated on the mainland side of the isthmus leading to Acadia, was taken after a short siege, and the smaller Fort Gaspereau fell without a struggle. There followed the harsh expulsion of the Acadians, simple people who had become political pawns and were now sent south into exile and misery.

Governor Shirley, held up by transport and supply problems, could not get beyond his base camp at Oswego. The enemy, thanks to Braddock's papers, knew all about his plans to attack Niagara. Shirley realised that unless he first took Frontenac, the French could cut off his retreat by capturing Oswego behind him, so he busied his men, including remnants of Braddock's forces, in strengthening Oswego.

The only real success, boosted beyond its merits to raise morale, was Johnson's campaign against Crown Point. His army was a disunited nation of 3,000 colonists and 300 Iroquois consisting of his beloved Mohawks and some Oneidas. Now appointed major-general, but without combat experience, the charming Johnson did a war-dance with his Indians and even disarmed the suspicions of his Bible-intoxicated New Englanders, the most God-fearing group since Cromwell's day, whose attitudes startled the New Yorkers and Rhode Island men present.

After the usual transport difficulties, he reached Lac du St Sacrement, which he was to name Lake George, later naming his two camps for the king's grandsons, Fort Edward and Fort William Henry. Meanwhile, the French under Dieskau were reinforcing Crown Point – once again the Braddock papers came in useful – then, with a disputed number of regulars, militia and Indians, perhaps 2,500 in all, he travelled down Lake Champlain and built Fort Ticonderoga.

Misled by a prisoner that Johnson had returned to his base at Albany, Dieskau pressed on with his army. He then learnt that the British were still in the area, and Johnson tried to ambush him with 500 men and his Indians, despite a warning from the Mohawk chief Hendrick who said: 'If they are to fight they are too few, if they are to die, they are too many.'

The wise old Indian was right, for 200 were killed, including Hendrick, and the survivors fled back in disorder to Johnson's camp at Lake George.

A fort was rapidly improvised from logs, boats and carts, and the advancing French met with a hail of bullets, the forerunner of similar blasts of fire against the British at Bunker Hill, New Orleans and elsewhere. The French and Indians broke and ran; Dieskau was captured and just saved by Johnson from being boiled and eaten in revenge for Hendrick's death.

Johnson did not pursue the shattered French, which has always been held against him by critics, even though pursuit might have ended in yet another British disaster. Instead, he nursed his wounded thigh, built Fort William Henry, and then, with his tired, sick and hungry men, he retired to the Hudson. He was made a baronet and granted £5,000 by Parliament.

Three naive but very important drawings by Lieutenant William Baillie, who in 1753 sketched members of his 13th Foot recruiting party in Birmingham. The 13th were not in America, but these lively if untutored drawings of battalion soldiers are rare representations of redcoats of the period. Note that the grenadier (left) has a GR cipher on his cartridge-box, and a picker and brush hanging from the belt just above it. 'Corporal Jones loading musket' (centre) shows hair tucked into hat, unusual spacing of lapel lace, and clearly drawn hook and eye on coat skirts. The vast number of tiny gaiter buttons must have caused some curses. The shirt cuff, visible on the right arm, seems to be closed with a link rather than a button; examples have been dug up in America. The right-hand sketch of Corporal Jones shows the lines of lace on the waistcoat, and the jaunty hat angle – to avoid accidents when shouldering arms. All the uniforms appear to be fairly crumpled, and rather tight. (Courtesy British Museum; and Light Infantry Museum, Taunton)

But the true significance of Lake George lay in the future. Mere provincials had licked French regulars. Dieskau said of them: 'In the morning they fought like good boys, about noon like men, and in the afternoon like devils.' Three of the devils were to become major generals against the British. Lake George was a warning of things to come.

MISMANAGEMENT AND MASSACRE

For the British 1755 had been a catastrophic year, and the following two years showed no improvement. Braddock's defeat led to an autumn of sheer terror on the frontier as French and Indian war-parties ravaged settlements and attacked lonely farmhouses, while colonial assemblies argued with their governors. Meanwhile, Colonel Dunbar, having hardly distinguished himself under Braddock, opted out by settling in Philadelphia for the winter.

Washington found himself commanding 1,500 Virginia Militia, virtually the only force to serve a 350-mile frontier in a situation quite out of control. The vast superiority in numbers of the British meant little in the face of the combination of wrangling colonists and French and Indian war-parties. The French ability to understand Indians was now paying off in terms of blood. It would be December 1755 before Pennsylvania would shake off its worthy Quaker shackles and prepare for war.

In the winter there was a lull as the enemy rested. Back in Britain, with a declared war clearly not far away, there was little sign of action. There were only 24,000 redcoats on the British establishment, with 13,000 more allocated to the colonies. A ray of hope was the granting of commissions to foreign Protestants in America, which led to the formation of the Royal American Regiment of Foot, the 60th, later the King's Royal Rifle Corps.

Various changes in uniform were taking place by 1760, which may be seen in these Sandby watercolours. These infantrymen have cream-coloured breeches, which were increasingly replacing the red type, and hats with a markedly higher cock at the front. One wears shorter gaiters with a stiff knee-piece. The cartridge-box was increased in size to take 36 rounds, and given a larger weather-proofing flap. (Reproduced by gracious permission of H.M. the Queen)

The spring of 1756 saw the judicial murder of Admiral Byng, who was made a scapegoat 'pour encourager les autres', as Voltaire observed. Meanwhile, with Britain seeking allies in Europe – Hanover and Prussia – the government sent £115,000 to Governor Shirley to help raise forces in New England for its defence. War was officially declared on 18 May, by which time a remarkable soldier, the Marquis de Montcalm, had reached Canada to replace the defeated Dieskau. There he encountered from the beginning the hostility of his superior, Vaudreuil, the governor-general, a colonial who saw no reason for the importation of a French regular. Their enmity was to benefit the British considerably. Montcalm brought with him able subordinates and 1,200 men. While the great Frenchman was discovering the disgracefully corrupt state of New France, the affairs of British America were being handed over to incompetents. The unfortunate Shirley, governor of Massachusetts, a man who served Britain and her colonies well, was due to be replaced by the Earl of Loudoun, but first he sent some inferior troops to Oswego, all that could be raised. More usefully, he appointed a veteran of Louisbourg, Major John

Bradstreet, a brilliant American soldier with a regular commission, to raise 2,000 armed boatmen. Their first achievement was to get supplies to Oswego despite French and Indian attacks.

In mid-July Loudoun arrived, soon after his even more useless subordinate, Major-General James Abercromby, and the equally feeble Colonel Daniel Webb. Shirley, hounded by his enemies, left in disgrace, while, unbelievably, an order accompanied Loudoun stating that even generals with provincial commissions could be outranked by mere regular majors. Better news was the arrival with Loudoun of the 35th and the 42nd Foot.

The rest of this miserable year was a chapter of calamities. Although Johnson managed to persuade many of the Iroquois to remain neutral this could not save Oswego from falling to Montcalm. The French captured over 1,600 prisoners, six ships, 113 cannon, plus ammunition, supplies and money, and silenced the fort. They had used Braddock's guns to help destroy it.

Hearing of the loss, a nervous Webb believed a rumour that Montcalm was advancing on him and fled to German Flats on the Mohawk. Actually, the war had petered out for the winter, with the British at Fort William Henry dying of disease in a stinking outpost facing the French at Ticonderoga (called by them Fort Carillon).

Another Sandby sketch, of an infantryman resting, c.1760. Again, note shorter gaiters and high, straight front to the hat. (Reproduced by gracious permission of H.M. the Queen)

That winter Newcastle, a master politician in the worst sense of the word, retired and the Duke of Devonshire took over. So, fortunately, did William Pitt. The British establishment was raised to 30,000 men, with 19,000 more for the colonies, plus 2,000 engineers and artillerymen. Fifteen line regiments were ordered to raise second battalions and Pitt – boldly, for it was only 12 years after the '45 rebellion – raised two regiments of Highlanders, Fraser's and Montgomery's. Among other signs of action were seven battalions ordered to North America and new drafts for regiments already there.

For all his faults, Loudoun should not have been burdened with the provincials, at their most selfish and insular at this critical time. Native Americans resented British troops being billeted on them, but expected the same troops to die for them.

Events of the 1757 campaign included a disappointment and a disaster. The former was an ill-mounted attack on Louisbourg, distinguished by late mustering of provincial troops, later reinforcements from Britain, and a late arrival by Loudoun at Halifax. Finally, the expedition found the great fortress heavily garrisoned and supported by a large French fleet, so sailed back to New York.

The disaster was the fall of Fort William Henry, where Lieutenant-Colonel Monro of the 35th Foot commanded over 2,000 redcoats and New Englanders, including sailors and mechanics. His men's health and morale was as alarming as the state of his 24 guns.

Montcalm had reached Fort Ticonderoga in July with 8,000 men, regulars, Canadians and Indians, and proceeded by land and water to besiege the British post. During the six-day siege the gutless Webb, though previously of good record, stayed put with 1,200 men at Fort Edward, a mere 14 miles away, and made no effort to summon several thousand troops south of him along the Hudson.

So it was that Monro and his disease-ridden troops, after losing 300 men (some of them killed by Braddock's guns), accepted Montcalm's surrender terms.

The terms were honourable and included an armed escort to Fort Edward, but the British failed to destroy the rum, which the Indians found and drank with disastrous results. The next morning the march began, with the Indians closing in ominously and demanding more rum. A massacre followed and a disputed number – 80 to 200 – of men, women and children were butchered before the French under Montcalm could restore order. The great Frenchman was not to blame. Both sides used Indians and knew the consequences of drink mixed with blood-lust. The survivors reached Fort Edward under escort and Webb called urgently for more men, who came up the Hudson. Montcalm, urged by his governor-general to advance, could not comply because of lack of supplies – back in Canada also there was a desperate food shortage – and because his Indians had headed for home with booty and captives. He returned to Fort Ticonderoga, having lost his one great chance of winning North America.

The winter of 1757–58 found morale in the colonies lower than ever, but though there were calamities to come, William Pitt was fully in command now. Even he was not to succeed at first, but everyone, even the most bloody-minded and insular provincial, now knew that there was a titan in command.

THE 1758 CAMPAIGNS

Pitt's plan for 1758 was a masterly one, but it was weakened by the impossibility of supervising it at a distance of 3,000 miles, the difficulties of communications, and by his exaggerated opinion of Abercromby. The new commander-in-chief of the army, the expatriate Huguenot, John Ligonier, selected Jeffrey Amherst to command the next attempt on Louisbourg. It was a good, if not inspired, choice. Admiral Boscawen was to command the fleet.

Under Amherst were 14,000 regulars. The grenadiers and light infantry, also the 42nd (the Black Watch), were to be commanded by Brigadier James Wolfe, whose earlier career will be found in the next chapter. Brigadier Lawrence commanded the 13th, 22nd, 35th and 45th Foot, also the 2nd Battalion, the Royal Americans – American troops under British discipline, paid for by Britain and some of them commanded by Swiss mercenaries. Colonel Whitmore commanded the 17th, 47th, 48th and 58th Regiments, also the 1st Royals and the 3rd Battalion, the Royal Americans.

Abercromby had 15,000 regulars and provincials and the finest young officer in the army, Lord Howe, as his second-in-command. Their plan was to head up Lake Champlain, while Brigadier John Forbes was to lead 6,000 men against Fort Duquesne.

Significantly, Pitt changed the official attitude to the colonies. Asking for 25,000 provincials, he said that Britain would provide food and shelter for them, only requiring the assemblies to raise, pay and clothe them. Also, senior provincial officers were no longer to be ordered about by mere regular striplings.

View, looking south-east, over the beautifully reconstructed Fort Ticonderoga, now a museum. The stone fort is of typical star-shape, with an inner courtyard or Place d'Armes where troops might assemble. There are barracks on south and west, four bastions, and two massive exterior defences – demi-lunes – on north and west; a square watch-tower rises on the east. (Courtesy Fort Ticonderoga Museum, New York)

The Louisbourg expedition did not leave Halifax until the end of May because of bad weather, but, finally, the transports set out escorted by 23 ships of the line. Their task was a daunting one, for to defend the fortress, the Chevalier de Drucour and the population of 4,000 had 3,000 regulars, plus Canadians, militia and Indians, 219 cannon and 17 mortars. The arrival of five ships of the line and seven frigates added 544 guns to the total.

The weather prevented the launch of boats from the transports for several days, but on 8 June the attack began. Feints were to be made by Lawrence and Whitmore, while the main attack rowed towards Freshwater Cove four miles from Louisbourg. This was led by Wolfe, who had with him five companies of grenadiers, 550 marksmen from various regiments, Fraser's Highlanders and provincial Rangers.

The French held their fire, then first artillery and next muskets from 1,000 entrenched men cut into the invaders. It looked like failure, but some of the light infantry had headed right against orders and landed on an unguarded section of rocks. After ordering them to withdraw, Wolfe realised his chance, changed his mind and was the first to land. Despite heavy losses of men and boats, he collected several hundred men, ordered them to fix bayonets, and led them against the French. The enemy fled, not even spiking their guns. Not until the fortress's cannon opened up to cover their panic-stricken troops did Wolfe halt.

The rest of the army came ashore and a siege began, giving Amherst, a less mercurial commander than Wolfe and less capable of improvising, a chance to shine. Bad weather and difficult terrain did not help the British, nor did Admiral Boscawen's perhaps prudent decision not to enter the harbour. The French dismantled a large battery on the north of the harbour opposite the fortress, into which they concentrated all their troops. Learning of this, Wolfe was ordered to move and bring both fortress and harbour under artillery fire.

By 23 July, the French were reduced, as Amherst noted, to firing 'all sorts of old Iron Nails on every occasion', but the well-entrenched British were not much troubled by the bombardment. The city was steadily reduced to rubble, and on 27 July the garrison capitulated, laying down firearms, colours, more than 200 cannon and surrendering vast amounts of stores. Over 5,000 men surrendered.

So fell Louisbourg, along with Cape Breton Island and Île St Jean (Prince Edward Island), and bells and bonfires sounded and blazed in America and Britain. Even the New England clergy indulged in paroxysms of loyalty to the Crown.

If the news from elsewhere had been better, Amherst could have pushed on towards Quebec, but Boscawen pointed out that such an operation could not succeed on its own. The Champlain campaign had collapsed because of Abercromby's gross blundering and the death of Howe.

The campaign had seemed promising enough. Before he left America, Loudoun had relaxed his European standards of warfare to the point of allowing Colonel Thomas Gage to raise a Ranger Regiment, the 80th, which was to model itself on Rogers' already famous Rangers. Abercromby, however, was a well-meaning, pleasant, slow-witted 'book' soldier of 52 (not to be confused with the famous Sir Ralph) whose lack of martial talent bordered on the phenomenal.

He had a fine army of 9,000 provincials and over 6,000 regulars, five regiments of them. This magnificent force, three times as strong as its opposition, had ample artillery support, supplies and 1,000 boats. It also had Lord Howe, grandson of George I and his mistress Baroness Kielmansegge, an officer in his mid-thirties. (His brothers were destined to be even more famous than he, William becoming commander-in-chief during the early part of the American Revolution, and Richard, Admiral 'Black Dick' Howe.)

Lord Howe was that rare being, the beau ideal of an English officer and gentleman. He had been made second-in-command to Abercromby to make up for the latter's suspected weaknesses. What set Howe apart from nearly every other officer was that by his bravery, skill, charm and brains he almost single-handedly overcame the colonists' hostility to British regular officers. He was 'the Idol of the Army', wrote one American. He scouted with Rogers, carried his own blanket and did his own washing without loss of respect, and he was as at home with the wildest backwoodsman as he was in a fashionable drawing-room. He rapidly mastered woodcraft by studying with those who knew it best, and he soon became the most liked and admired British soldier ever to serve alongside Americans.

He worked to transform his own men. The long skirts of their jackets were shorn off, so were their pigtails; musket barrels were browned to prevent glitter; pipeclay and leather stocks were banned. Howe also ordered officers to live rough, making them cut down their own baggage, do their own washing as he did, and eat more simply. Morale soared in the ranks.

On 5 July the expedition embarked from its camp by the ruins of Fort William Henry in its fleet of bateaux, whale-boats and artillery flatboats. Bands played as the armada moved north. In the van were Rogers' and Gage's Rangers and Howe's 55th Foot. Men from Britain, New York, New England, New Jersey and Rhode Island sailed to win Canada from Montcalm. The French general had 3,500 men and his position at Fort Ticonderoga seemed serious. Fortunately for the French, the British advance had been held back by the slow assembling of the provincials, but now, with the British advancing up the lake, Montcalm withdrew his outposts in the fort's perimeter and ordered the fortifications to be strengthened. A defence line of tree trunks and earth was frantically built, and trees were felled round the fort with the branches facing the expected line of attack.

Montcalm had little more than a week's supplies. His retreat could have been cut off if Abercromby had sent a force to control the narrows between the two lakes, but he had one stroke of luck, the arrival of 400 regulars and the same number of Canadians, sent by the governor-general.

Charming drawing showing officers of the Independent Companies dining – or rather wining – with friends. The officer at left wears his sash, and his lapels buttoned across; the two facing us have theirs buttoned back. (Courtesy the Henry Francis du Pont Winterthur Museum)

Abercromby's men landed at 10 a.m. on the morning of 6 July, and by noon his whole army had disembarked. The French had destroyed the bridge across the channel dividing the lakes and it was decided to advance up the western bank and attack the fort from the rear. Rogers went ahead to scout, with the rest of the force trying to follow but getting lost in the forest. Then came a major tragedy. Howe, with some Rangers, ran into a French scouting party and a fierce skirmish followed. It was a small-scale affair with great consequences, for Howe was shot through the heart.

The whole army was shattered by the loss, as were Americans generally. Abercromby was not only shaken – he promptly went to pieces. Despite advice to attack the enemy on the flank having first wrecked their breastworks with cannon fire, he decided on 8 July to attack head-on with the bayonet. Carefully stationing himself a mile and a half away, he sent his men against the completed breastworks.

Battalion after battalion was sacrificed, cut to pieces by musketry and grapeshot. First in were the Rangers and light infantry, then came the 42nd and the 55th. The desperate attack of the Black Watch was the most famous of the many hopeless assaults that were launched on the French positions. For a full hour the Scots tried to storm the breastworks, hacking their way with broadswords and trying to shoot an enemy they could not see, but finally even these bravest of the brave – what was left of them – had to fall back.

Abercromby now surpassed himself. He sent his men in again and there followed one of the most valiant attempts in the history of arms to storm an impregnable position. It failed, as it was bound to; then, with the French almost out of ammunition, Abercromby ordered a retreat, and even the reluctant Highlanders finally obeyed. Montcalm, who had inspired his men greatly, had lost about 400 of them; 1,600 regulars fell,

Models of the flat-bottomed landing barges used to transport troops at Quebec. In the 'manned' model, note naval officer at the tiller, and drummer in bows, with landing-party of grenadiers. (National Maritime Museum, Greenwich)

314 men of the Black Watch being killed and 334 wounded, while the provincials lost 334 men. The wretched Abercromby partly blamed the provincials for the disaster and wished to retreat at once to Albany, but, fortunately, he managed to force himself to entrench his men once again at the foot of Lake George.

Montcalm had saved Canada with Abercromby's help, and now suffered, not from the British, but from his own governor-general who urged him vainly to advance with his tiny force. The British effort in 1758 seemed little better than in previous years, Louisbourg apart, but in August things improved. In 1757, Lieutenant-Colonel Bradstreet had been eager to attack Fort Frontenac (now Kingston, Ontario), the French supply base for their western outposts. Now, in 1758, he got his chance, leading a force of over 2,500 men, provincials, militia and 157 Royal Americans.

They passed the ruins of Oswego and sailed across Lake Ontario, avoiding action with three French ships, and appeared at Fort Frontenac on 25 August to find only 110 men there, plus nine ships and 60 cannon. All fell easily into Bradstreet's hands before Vaudreuil could rush reinforcements to the fort, which was then destroyed. This major provincial triumph lost the French control of Lake Ontario.

The other campaign, too, was a success, though its leader, Brigadier John Forbes, did not survive it. He was a fine Scottish soldier in his 60s, the colonel of the 17th Foot. He believed in studying 'the art of warr from the enemy, Indians or anything else who have seen the country and warr carried on in it'. Reaching Philadelphia in April 1758, he ran into the by now traditional difficulties that had afflicted Braddock earlier.

He finally mustered some 1,600 men, including Montgomery's Highlanders, a battalion of Royal Americans under a Swiss soldier, Henry Bouquet, and provincials from all the central colonies, including a large body of Virginians, and many southern Indians.

His route to Fort Duquesne was the shortest and best, taken against the advice of land-hungry Americans of the Ohio Company who wanted to take Braddock's old road, repair it and turn it into a free short-cut to their would-be possessions. One of those who urged this was Washington, whose motives may or may not have been disinterested. He had endured several years of frontier warfare, still without a regular commission, but he served Forbes loyally with his Virginian provincials. On the march Forbes was hit by severe dysentery, which gradually wrecked his health altogether, and he had to be carried on a litter between two horses.

The road was hacked out of the forest, forts were built at regular intervals, but progress was slow. Then an ambitious junior officer caused a disaster. Major James Grant, commanding 800 Highlanders and Virginians, got permission from Bouquet, leading the vanguard, to try to take Fort Duquesne by a night attack. Though he got within a mile of the fort, his men became lost and the French attacked them. Three hundred

1: Corporal, Battalion Company, 45th Foot, 1750s
2: Grenadier, 15th Foot (Amherst's)
3: Private, Battalion Company, 43rd Regiment of Foot, marching order, 1750s
4: Sergeant, Battalion Company, 27th (Inniskilling) Regiment of Foot, 1750s

A

1: Private, Virginia Regiment, 1755
2: Petty Officer, Royal Navy, 1755
3: Staff Officer, 1755
4: Private, Battalion Company,
   48th Regiment of Foot, 1755
5: Private, Battalion Company,
   44th Regiment of Foot, 1755

1: Soldier of the Independent Companies, 1755
2: Private, the Virginia Regiment, 1755–62
3: Typical campaign dress
4: Officer, New Jersey 'Blues'
5: Officers, 2nd Connecticut Regiment, 1758

C

1: Officer, Rogers' Rangers
2: Ranger, His Majesty's Independent Companies of
   American Rangers, 1758
3: Ranger, later 1750s
4: Rogers' Rangers, Stockbridge Indians
5: Rangers, 1758-61

D

1: Senior Officer, 1st or Royal Regiment of Foot, late 1750s
2: Officer, Grenadier Company, 46th Regiment of Foot
3: Infantry Officer in field dress, 1758
4: Fifer, Drummer, 35th Foot, late 1750s

E

1: Private, 80th Regiment of Light Armed Foot
   (Gage's Light Infantry), 1758
2: Light Infantrymen, 1759
3: Officer, 40th Foot, 1758-59
4: Grenadier, 60th (Royal American) Regiment of
   Foot, 1759
5: Soldiers, 55th Foot, 1758

1: Officer, Royal Artillery, 1759
2: Captain of over three years' seniority, Royal Navy
3: Major-General James Wolfe, 1759
4: Privates, Grenadier Company.
Sergeant, Battalion Company, 78th Foot
(Fraser's Highlanders), 1757–63

G

1: Sergeant, 58th Regiment of Foot, winter dress,
late 1750s
2: Grenadier, 28th Regiment, winter dress
3: Private, 17th Regiment, winter dress, 1759
4: Officers and men in winter dress

H

were killed and wounded, and a panic-stricken rout only ended at the base camp. Bouquet halted the fugitives and, not being a Dunbar, held his own.

British morale was made lower by rain and mud, but in late November the troops near Fort Duquesne learnt from a prisoner that the French were abandoning the fort. Within a mile of the fort the forest suddenly echoed with the sound of explosions: the tiny garrison – only 200 strong now – was burning it down. The British marched in the next day, 25 November.

Forbes left a small garrison and named the fort 'Pittsborough', which was soon shortened to Pitt.

An impression of Quebec after British bombardment. (Public Archives of Canada}

Helped by Bradstreet's success to the north, he had achieved a major triumph, but he was now a dying man. Leaving Bouquet in charge of building Fort Pitt (and Washington to go home and marry a rich widow, Martha, and retire from soldiering for 17 years) Forbes was carried home to die a hero in Philadelphia. So ended a year of triumphs ruined in part by one appalling tragedy. Pitt sacked Abercromby, and Amherst took his place for the 1759 campaign. But in November 1758, just before Fort Duquesne fell, young James Wolfe, already racked with ill health, had returned to London from Louisbourg to find himself a popular hero.

WITH WOLFE TO QUEBEC

James Wolfe was born at Westerham in Kent in 1727. He was of Irish and Yorkshire descent, a potent mixture for a soldier, and his father had risen to be a lieutenant-colonel under Marlborough. Only ill health prevented the boy accompanying him to the Siege of Cartagena in 1740; but the next year, young Wolfe became a second lieutenant of Marines.

Being a martyr to seasickness, it was lucky that he transferred to the l2th Foot. His first battle was Dettingen, by which time he was 16 and already an adjutant. His horse was shot under him and the Duke of Cumberland noted his efforts, a good start for a born soldier.

He fought at Culloden and on at least one occasion showed himself more ruthless than he need have been in 'pacifying' the Highlands. He cared deeply about his duty, tried to live on his pay, and began his endless run of ill health as he brooded about his profession and his lonely garrison life. Though he fought in the Netherlands in 1747, most of his pre-American career was spent in Scotland, where he never ceased trying to improve himself, even hiring a mathematics tutor. His temper was explosive and sudden, his nature warm and impetuous and sometimes arrogant, and his military genius was a mixture of dash and diligent attention to detail. As many have noted, he had much in common with Nelson, including the ability to inspire loyalty in those below him. When his hour came at a very early age, he was a seasoned veteran who had trained his men to such a peak of efficiency that even his least observant superiors noted it.

When Wolfe finally left Scotland in 1753, he was a lieutenant-colonel cursed by 'the stone' and rheumatism. The 20th, currently his regiment, was to be four years in the south. He had to endure reading about the

Watercolour of James Wolfe painted by George Townshend in 1759. (McCord Museum, Canada)

bungling of others in North America until, in 1757, he was made quartermaster-general of the force sent against Rochefort, the first of his three major amphibious expeditions. This abortive effort led to the court martial of its leader, Sir John Mordaunt, who, in modern parlance, was 'past it'. Only two senior officers came out of the feebly conducted expedition well: Wolfe, and Captain Richard Howe, later, a famous admiral .

At the inquiry into the fiasco, Wolfe's performance on the witness stand was widely admired. He summed up his colleagues privately to a friend: 'There never was people collected together so unfit for the business they were sent upon – dilatory, ignorant, irresolute, and some grains of a very unmanly quality and very unsoldierlike or unsailorlike'. He excepted Howe.

The king got to hear of Wolfe's efforts and promoted him colonel. Wolfe departed for the Louisbourg campaign, and on his return to London in November 1758 was treated as a hero.

In December, Pitt summoned Wolfe and offered him the command of the expedition up the St Lawrence to take Quebec. He was to be a major-general – local American rank – and he was not quite 32.

For Newcastle, the choice of such a man on grounds of sheer merit was too much. He rushed to George II to complain, but the veteran of Dettingen admired young Wolfe. When informed that the fellow was mad, he made his immortal reply: 'Mad is he? Then I hope he will bite some of my other generals!'

In America, Amherst had heard he was to be commander-in-chief on the previous 9 November. He had 23 under-strength battalions of regulars and many promises of provincial troops, whose numbers finally reached 12,000 in all.

Pitt's plan was once again a four-pronged one. Apart from Amherst's campaign to the north and Wolfe's up the St Lawrence, Brigadier Stanwix was to reinforce Fort Pitt, and Brigadier Prideaux, with Sir William Johnson as his second-in-command, was to take Fort Niagara, then head eastwards down the St Lawrence.

This last campaign was to divide the Canadians from their people in the west and wreck plans to retake Fort Pitt. Prideaux had two regular regiments, a battalion of Royal Americans, over 3,000 provincials; and thanks to Johnson, 900 previously neutral Iroquois joined the expedition.

The force reached Niagara and besieged the fort. Prideaux was killed early in the siege and Johnson, provincial that he was, took over with no complaints from the regulars. It was to him that the great prize fell on 25 July; a little-remembered victory today, but almost as significant a one as Quebec.

Amherst was a slower mover. In late June, he rebuilt Fort William Henry and, in late July, took a deserted Fort Ticonderoga after a stubborn defence by the French rearguard. Then he settled down to rebuild the fort and construct ships to dominate Lake Champlain. The French were now very much on the defensive, and everything depended on Wolfe.

His three aristocratic brigadiers were Robert Monckton of Acadia fame; George Murray, a brave, ambitious, envious soldier; and George Townshend, the malicious, sullen, arrogant nephew of the Duke of

Newcastle, but undeniably brave and clever and, not least, a good artist and caricaturist. He was three years older than Wolfe. There were two staff officers: the Quartermaster-General, Guy Carleton, later the saviour of Canada, and Isaac Barré, the Adjutant-General, and the son of a Huguenot. The Chief Engineer was Major Patrick Mackellar, who had been with Braddock, been captured, taken to Quebec, and exchanged complete with a perfect description of the city and its defences in his head.

On the naval side, Wolfe could not have been luckier. Vice-Admiral Sir Charles Saunders, a protégé of Anson's, was the finest type of naval officer. His second-in-command, Rear-Admiral Durell, was less able, but the number three, Rear-Admiral Charles Holmes, was a fine sailor. Also under Saunders were two men destined respectively to fame and immortality: John Jervis, later Lord St Vincent, and James Cook, the humbly born Yorkshireman later to become the greatest of all navigators.

The fleet was a fine one; there were three large ships of the line, including Saunders' 90-gun *Neptune*, a number of smaller ships of the line, plus frigates, sloops, fire-ships, bomb-ketches and 119 supply and ordnance ships.

Wolfe's army was only slightly less remarkable, less so because the originally planned 12,000 had been reduced to 8,500 by sickness, desertions and other causes. On 6 June 1759, an army almost wholly made up of regulars sailed from Louisbourg. There were no cavalry, but three companies of artillery, who could be supported by guns from the ships, and six companies of Rangers, who were characterised at first by Wolfe, an ardent anti-American from a military point of view, as the worst soldiers in the universe.

His regiments were the 15th, 28th, 35th, 43rd, 47th, 48th and 58th[1]. There were also Fraser's battalion of Highlanders, the 78th,[2] whose officers were much admired by Wolfe, and the 2nd and 3rd Battalions of the Royal American Regiment. These were the men determined – in the words of Sergeant Ned Botwood, the soldier-versifier of the 47th – to give the French 'hot stuff'.

There were grenadier companies from each of the regiments and a small corps of light infantry, and later 300 colonial pioneers were to arrive for the siege.

Wolfe followed Lord Howe's sensible reforms with some of his own. He might dislike and despise Indians, but he could order knapsacks to be carried higher and fastened with 'a scrap of web over the shoulder, as the Indians carry their packs'. Extra pockets for musket balls and flints were sewn on, scouts' coats were made freer and the lace of the cuffs abolished. The grenadier companies' mitre caps were retained, but the light infantry's hats were turned into caps 'with as much black cloth added under his chin' to 'keep him warm when he lies down'.

A fine example of a contemporary officer's uniform – that of Captain Thomas Plumbe of the Royal Lancashire Militia, c.1760. Coat, waistcoat and breeches are red, the former two items fully and the latter partly lined with blue. The collar is lined with blue velvet, the lace is all gold and the buttons copper-gilt. Lapels can be buttoned back and the coat closed with cloth-covered buttons on a red fly. All edges are 'raw'. The unlined white linen gaiters have 29 horn buttons; they are cut to the shape of the leg and stitched up the back, with inset sections over the foot, and linen tapes underneath. (Lancashire Museum, G. A. Embleton)

---

1. 15th Foot, later the East Yorkshire Regiment. 28th Foot, later the Gloucestershire Regiment. 35th Foot, later the Royal Sussex Regiment. 43rd Foot, later the Oxfordshire and Buckinghamshire Light Infantry (1st Battalion). 47th Foot, later the North Lancashire Regiment (1st Battalion). 48th Foot, later the Northamptonshire Regiment (1st Battalion). 58th Foot, later the Northamptonshire Regiment (2nd Battalion).

2. The 78th Highlanders were a temporary unit serving only in the Seven Years War; though raised once again in 1778, and eventually becoming the Seaforth Highlanders, there is no direct link.

Meanwhile, the French had been betrayed by their own government. It was bad enough that the governor-general and commander-in-chief were at loggerheads, but far worse, that Montcalm's messenger to France, Bougainville, could not make her rulers see beyond Europe. He returned to Canada with about 400 men and – something at least – instructions that military decisions were to be made by Montcalm. He also carried an intercepted letter revealing Pitt's plans, so Montcalm was able to revise his. But, like everyone else, he believed that the British could not sail up the St Lawrence, which was considered by Frenchmen to be a navigational nightmare. For the defence of the whole country he could only muster some 16,000 men, about 3,000 of them regulars, but with desertions and leave for farming, the total was more like 11,000. In his final encounter at Quebec with Wolfe, both sides were to have about 4,500 men.

By 26 June, Wolfe's army had been transported up the St Lawrence and its commander had landed on the Île d'Orleans, four miles from Quebec. It had been a magnificent feat of seamanship, though British sailors did not think it so. 'Damn me,' roared Captain Killick, master of the transport *Goodwill*, at a Canadian pilot, 'I'll convince you that an Englishman shall go where a Frenchman dare not show his nose!' Then, having cleared a difficult passage, he claimed: 'Damn me if there aren't a thousand places on the Thames more hazardous than this.' The French were stunned.

Wolfe could now see Quebec and also the Beauport Lines stretching eight miles eastwards from the city. Monckton was at once sent to take Point Levis, downstream from Quebec on the southern bank of the river, before the French realised its importance. On the 28th, the French tried floating fire-ships downstream on Saunders' ships, but bungled the job, the fire-ships being set alight too soon. Saunders then anchored under the lee of Point Levis. British artillery was placed two miles west of it in easy range of the citadel, and, on 9 July, Wolfe sent troops east of the Falls of Montmorenci, which did not lure Montcalm out. On the 27th, the French made another attack with fire-ships but again they failed, and, four days later, it was the turn for British action.

This was Wolfe's misconceived attack on the Beauport Lines, a combined operation which failed because of faulty reconnaissance. Though the shallows of the Beauport Bank had been found, which prevented ships getting close in, a ledge short of the flats had not. So the landings went in at intervals instead of in one major assault. The grenadiers in particular suffered heavy casualties from cannon and 'Small shot like showers of hail' as they tried to climb the slope, until a rainstorm soaked the ammunition of both sides. Wolfe ordered a withdrawal after his grenadiers and marines had lost 500 officers and men. Sergeant Ned Botwood, too, fell in this action. 'Come, each death-dealing dog who dares venture his neck, Come, follow the hero that goes to Quebec', he had written in his magnificent doggerel poem, but for once the hero had blundered.

A lull occurred during which Wolfe tried to dishearten the Canadians by destroying all nearby settlements, hoping he would cause the militia to desert. Spasmodic guerrilla warfare had been going on for some time in a minor, but savage way, with the Rangers using their scalping knives as well as the Indians and Canadians until Wolfe objected, and with the

Gabriel Christie, captain and major in the 48th Foot from 1754 to 1762, was at Ticonderoga in 1759. He wears a scarlet regimental coat, faced buff, a buff waistcoat, and gold lace and buttons. His insignia of rank is a shoulder knot of two parallel rows of lace forming a shoulder-strap ending in a bow with a flattened knot, with a loop and tail hanging down the arm. (Courtesy the Curator, Chateau de Ramezay)

Indians complaining to the French that the British were harder to kill than in Braddock's day.

Meanwhile, Admiral Saunders had sent several vessels upstream and troops had landed, severing communications between Quebec and Montreal, but stalemate followed, punctuated by bombardment of the city. It seemed impossible to cross the Montmorenci upstream because of its defences, and farther west the Charles River was a further barrier to be overcome, even supposing the Montmorenci were forced.

In late August, Wolfe's health finally broke down and he lay sick, frustrated and depressed in his camp on the east bank of the Montmorenci. His three brigadiers took over and it was they who suggested a landing upstream of Quebec. Reconnaissance from the south bank led Wolfe to choose a cove called the Anse de Foulon at the foot of near vertical cliffs (they are far less so today) which were, however, scalable. The resourceful Captain Robert Stobo, who had been at Fort Necessity, and had now escaped from Quebec, where for a time he had been on parole, agreed with this choice of landing-place. Even before his arrival in the St Lawrence, Wolfe had hoped to land above the city, but illness seems to have clouded his judgement, leading to his subordinates actually putting up the plan.

On 12 September, British intelligence reported that provision ships would try to reach Quebec on the next ebb tide, just the cover needed to help the new plan to success. At 1 a.m. on 13 September two lanterns were swung to the maintop of HMS *Sutherland*, the signal for Wolfe and 1,700 men aboard 30 landing-craft to start their hazardous adventure. In the first six boats were William Howe's light infantry, with Captain Delaune of the 47th beside Howe in the leading boat. Wolfe was up with the leaders, along with the 28th, 43rd, 47th and 58th Regiments, also the Highlanders and Royal Americans. 1,900 were to follow later, including the 15th, 78th and 35th, more light infantry, the remainder of the Royal Americans and the Louisbourg Grenadiers.

The weather was good and it was a starlit night, but that did not make a river with a six-knot tide and swollen by rains, easy to navigate. Ships opposite Beauport made a feint attack, and Montcalm massed most of his men there to ward it off.

As the boats passed close to the shore on the way to the landing-place, the story goes that French sentries challenged them with 'Who goes there?' One version has it that Captain Donald McDonald, a Jacobite in his time who had served in France, answered: 'La France.' 'Which regiment?' he was asked. 'The Queen's,' he replied in French. Another sentry challenged him and he said the boats were the provision ships and was believed. There was no guard at the landing-place. It was 4 o'clock in the morning.

The cliffs rose 175 feet above the invaders, some of whom scrambled up as best they could, others using the only path. In the dark it was a

The Death of Wolfe by Edward Penny, c.1764. In an earlier, more realistic version of this painting Penny showed the battle-line in the distance, having advanced from the scene of Wolfe's fall. He took great trouble to paint the figures accurately, however, and the costumes are worth careful study. He was advised by an eye-witness, Volunteer Henderson of the Louisbourg Grenadiers. (Courtesy The Ashmolean Museum, Oxford)

tricky climb, but the first men up, including Howe, Delaune and some light infantry, soon overpowered the post at the top, which was slackly held, and let out a hurrah. Wolfe was at his best in the complicated situation which demanded organisation and inspiration of a high order; and before sun-up, the whole of his 4,500-strong force was on the Heights of Abraham and moving on to the plain. Captain Chads, who had led the convoy to its destination, having been selected as the best boat navigator in the fleet, could relax. It was up to the army now.

There was a moment when guns to the west made Wolfe believe that Bougainville's forces, eight miles upstream, were approaching, and he ordered that troops not yet disembarked should remain in their boats. Fortunately, Barré had disobeyed him.

Wolfe's position was dangerous. Though Montcalm's line of battle was to be numerically the same, the French had Canadians and Indians, as well as Bougainville, as a possible threat; but so brilliant had the operation been that Wolfe had all the time he needed to assemble his battle-line, first with his troops with their backs to the river, then, after a personal reconnaissance, deployed on open ground. It was an ideal position for his army, which was entirely made up of regulars drilled to his own standard and ready to use their massive fire-power to maximum effect. Only his flanks were open to attack and, before Montcalm arrived, Canadians and Indians were causing some nuisance on the left flank.

Showers were falling as Wolfe's magnificent thin red line, standing two deep, its files a yard apart with more than 40 yards between each battalion, took up its battle order. From right to left of the line were the

Louisbourg Grenadiers with Wolfe at their head, the 28th, 43rd, 78th, 58th and 15th Foot. The Royal Americans and the 48th were in reserve, while Howe's men guarded the flanks and the rear. The Highlanders looked splendidly conspicuous in the centre in their kilts.

When the news was brought to Montcalm, he decided that only a small party had landed, but, somewhat alarmed, he galloped off on his black charger to be stunned by what he saw; a British army, drawn up for battle and motionless. It was 6.30 a.m.

Without surprise on its side, Wolfe's army might well have been defeated, but as it was, the surprise was complete. De Vergor, who had commanded the post at the top of the cliffs, had an appalling record, which was made worse that night because he had allowed most of his men to go home for the harvest. On such small things can the fate of continents depend.

Not until 9.30 a.m. were the two battle-lines finally drawn up, the French having the regiments of Bearn and La Sarre on the right, the troops of Guyenne and Languedoc on the left. The battle began at 10 a.m. Montcalm has been criticised for not waiting for Bougainville and his men (probably rightly) but he wanted to dislodge the British before they were firmly established. He did not realise that they already were. As for Wolfe, he had to force an action and, fortunately, action came on his terms.

Montcalm thought that the British were already entrenched, but they were merely down on the ground to avoid the now very troublesome fire from Canadians and Indians on the flanks, who were being dealt with by the British skirmishers. But this was a mere side-show. Now the French, fired on by artillery dragged up the cliffs, began to advance and the redcoats rose up to await them.

The French came on at a run, which at once broke their lines, then fired too soon, the Canadians among them flinging themselves to the ground to reload. They decided to retreat rather than face a British volley with its following bayonet charge, but the French regulars continued to advance as the British stood motionless, each redcoat with his Brown Bess at the ready. The orders had been given: 'Handle cartridge', 'Prime', 'Load', 'Draw ramrod', 'Return ramrods', 'Make ready', 'Present'. Now only 'Give fire' remained.

The order came when the French were 40 yards away, and the volley which followed, so Sir John Fortescue wrote, was the most perfect ever fired on a battlefield. In the centre of the British line it was like a single shot, only less so on the right and left, and it won Canada.

There was another volley, and the smoke rose to reveal the ruin of an army. Then came the order to charge and a great cheer went up. The British surged forward with bayonets and claymores as Montcalm's men fled. Wolfe, already injured in the wrist, was now struck in the groin and the chest, as he led the Louisbourg Grenadiers and the 35th forward, but his work – the climax of years of preparation and training – was done.

He was laid down, refusing a surgeon because 'It is needless; it is all over with me.' 'They run,' cried someone. 'Who runs?' asked the dying man urgently. 'The enemy run. Egad, they give way everywhere,' was the reply. Wolfe gave his final orders to cut off the fugitives, then, smiling, said: 'Now, God be praised, I will die in peace.' A moment later, as Parkman wrote, 'his gallant soul had fled'.

The Death of Wolfe by Benjamin West, c.1770. West was more concerned with dramatic effect than historical accuracy, and many of the people depicted were not even in America, let alone at Wolfe's side; there is a strong suggestion that places in this prestigious scene were obtainable from the artist for a financial consideration! Several men who were definitely with Wolfe at the end are not shown. Considering Wolfe's lively dislike of Indians, the inclusion of one here is most unconvincing. The costume is a mixture of 1750s and 1770s styles. Wolfe's clothes were sketched by a staff officer. (Courtesy the National Gallery of Canada, Ottawa)

The French retreat was a rout from the first, so 'horrid' and 'abominable' in the words of a survivor that Townshend, the new commander, failed to bottle up the enemy along the shore at Beauport. Many escaped towards Montreal, and others only survived because the town was so near. Too late, Bougainville appeared to help, summed up the situation, and retreated westwards.

Townshend, Wolfe's bitterest critic, could not cope with a situation which needed improvisation of a high order, always Wolfe's strong point. Montcalm, too, had been mortally wounded, and Townshend contented himself with besieging Quebec. Five hundred French had died and 350 been taken prisoner, while the British had lost nine officers and 49 men, with nearly 600 wounded. Montcalm died on the 14th and the city capitulated on the 18th. Bougainville was now on his way back to Quebec with better troops than had fought there, but it was too late. The capital of New France and the birthplace of Canada was in British hands.

THE FALL OF NEW FRANCE

If Quebec had fallen, Canada had yet finally to be won. Amherst heard about the victory while still at Crown Point. His ponderous advance was not helped by disease and desertions, but the sufferers were Brigadier Murray's garrison of 7,500 men who had been left in Quebec when the fleet had had to sail away for the winter because of the St Lawrence ice. The redcoats endured bitter months which left more than half of them unfit for duty.

In April 1760, the new French commander, De Levis, tried to recapture Quebec before the ice broke and the navy could return. A second, very severe battle was fought on the Plains of Abraham, which Murray did not lose for he was able to retreat safely into the citadel, while the French, being without siege guns, could do nothing to follow up their advantage. The defences were strengthened, officers working with their men to place 150 guns on the walls; then, on 9 May, the fleet arrived, De Levis was in full retreat and Quebec was saved.

Amherst heard the news from the north and at last, in the summer, he moved. By 24 August, Murray had reached a point only nine leagues from Montreal, while Brigadier Haviland was closing in on the city via the Richelieu River. Amherst by now was leading eight under-strength battalions of 6,000 regulars, plus 500 provincials, down the St Lawrence, and, by 6 September, the three armies were besieging the city, 17,000 men against Vaudreuil's 2,500 regulars. Canada's Indians had seen that it was time to stop supporting the French and had made peace.

The end came on 9 September, and with it a century and a half during which the outnumbered French and Canadians had so often had the best of the matter in the fight with the English. They had gradually been worn down by lack of support at home, British sea power, intrigue and corruption in New France and, finally, by determined British efforts. The Treaty of Paris finished both the Seven Years' War and also its gory, dramatic offshoot, the French and Indian War.

Long before this, James Wolfe had met his end in the hour of victory. Townshend had done his best to underplay his dead commander's part in that victory, but his malicious efforts were drowned in a sea of acclamation. Montcalm, too, suffered denigration after his death, at the hands of his governor-general, but history has seen to it that only the names of victor and vanquished live on, not the pygmies who assailed them.

As for the redcoats, having won a victory which freed the colonies from the French menace and soon had them thinking about freedom themselves, they suffered the usual fate of British soldiers after a war. While some of them found themselves in action against Pontiac, whose rebellion of 1763 was the last really dangerous Indian uprising, others were 'axed' as an economy measure. The fact that Pontiac proved how brittle was the peace in North America made no difference. Soon the colonists, the French menace gone, forgot their gratitude to the men who had saved them; soon the mere sight of a redcoat would be anathema to many Americans. The redcoats would be in America in strength again, and this time it would be to fight a war that, for all their traditional bravery, won them no battle honours to set below Quebec.

BIBLIOGRAPHY

Bulletin of the Company of Military Historians
Corbett, Sir Julian, *England and the Seven Years' War* (1907) .
Cuneo , John R., *Robert Rogers of the Rangers* (1959).
Fregault, Guy, *Canada: The War of the Conquest.* Translated by Margaret M. Cameron (1969).
Grinnell-Milne, Duncan, *Mad, is he? The Character and Achievement of James Wolfe* (1963).
Hamilton, Charles (Ed.), *Braddock's Defeat* (1959).
Hargreaves, Reginald, *The Bloodybacks* (1968).
Hibbert, Christopher, *Wolfe at Quebec* (1959).
Knox, Captain John, *An Historical Journal of the Campaigns in North America.* Edited by A. G. Doughty in three vols., 1914-16 (1769).
Journal for the Society of Army Historical Research
Lawson, C. P., *The Uniforms of the British Army* (London 1961)
Lloyd, Christopher, *The Capture of Quebec* (1959).
Parkman, Francis, *Montcalm and Wolfe* (1884).
Richards, Frederick B., *The Black Watch at Ticonderoga and Major Duncan Campbell of Inverawe* (New York Historical Association).
Stacey, C. P., *Quebec 1759* (1959).
Warner, Oliver, *With Wolfe to Quebec* (1972).

THE PLATES

Many of the details of the uniforms illustrated here can only be the subject of educated guesswork, and the author and illustrator have not shrunk from such guesswork after carefully examining all available contemporary material. They make no apology for this, but are conscious that any illustration reconstructed from a written description is vulnerable to alternative interpretations. They hope that anyone possessing more positive information may be prompted to put it into print.

Information on regimental life, uniforms and equipment of this period is very scarce; it is limited to portraits of officers and a few sketches and paintings, and to regimental records and order books, inspections returns, and the Royal Clothing Warrant (sic). The finest pictorial record of the clothing of other ranks is the series of paintings by David Morier, now in the Royal Collection at Windsor. The author and artist know of no contemporary illustration of other ranks' dress while on service in North America, and with the exception of a few mitre caps, know of no surviving items of their uniforms. Few among even the officers left journals; and although NCOs were expected to be able to write and many soldiers were literate, only the most fragmentary diaries and letters of common soldiers have come down to us. In this attempt to bring Wolfe's men to life, we have drawn on material dealing with the organisation and control of the Army and the life of the soldier at home in Britain or on service in Europe as well as in North America.

Commanders of regiments were very much like ships' captains at that time; by their interest and enthusiasm, or lack of it, they set the tone of their battalions. Dress, equipment, and the quality of recruits varied enormously. Some regiments were poor in every respect – the officers rarely present, the NCOs worthless, and the uniforms worn out. In others genuine esprit de corps was cultivated; and inspecting generals, who regularly reported on the regiments and attempted to enforce adherence to the Royal Warrants and Sealed Patterns, might compliment a colonel on a fine body of men but complain about minor alterations to regulation uniform adopted to 'cut a dash'.

PLATE A

A1: Corporal, Battalion Company, 45th Foot, 1750s
Corporals were distinguished by a knot of white or regimental tape on the right shoulder (its origin obscure, but probably deriving from the decorative 'points' of the Medieval period); otherwise this is the basic dress of all the battalion or 'hat' men (a nickname distinguishing them from the grenadiers with their mitre caps). The brick-red coat, waistcoat and breeches were cut after the civilian fashion of the day, fully lined in the regimental colour which showed at the cuffs, lapels and skirts. (Coats were apparently worn inside out while at sea). The buttonholes and various edges of the coat and waistcoat were decorated and reinforced with a woven tape – 'lace' with a regimentally distinctive pattern of coloured lines, worms or shapes. The coarse felt-like woollen coat material was cut with a raw, unhemmed edge. Coats were renewed each year, and when the new issue arrived, all tailors, and other soldiers handy with needle and thread, were excused other duties and turned to fitting

their fellow soldiers. Each man paid the tailor one shilling for turning his last year's coat into a waistcoat (and perhaps breeches), and eightpence for fitting his 'small-clothes'. 'Foraging caps' were made from left-overs.

White 'rollers' or neckcloths were worn, and woollen stockings. Rounded buckles were preferred as they did not cut into the shoes which were cut straight so as to fit either foot. Uniform buttons were usually plain pewter, although some regiments wore yellow metal. In 1752 it was ordered that the colour should follow the gold or silver of the officers' lace in each regiment. Some regiments wore buttons marked with the regimental number, and in 1767 this became regulation for all. Hair was powdered – with flour – for ceremonials and parades. It was usually tucked up under the hat, and wigs were only worn by bald men, and some officers.

A2: Grenadier, 15th Foot (Amherst's); in America, 1758–67
Grenadiers were distinguished by their tall mitre caps, match-cases, and 'wings' – shoulder decorations of red cloth bound with regimental lace. (In 1751 Morier shows only 19 regiments wearing wings, but in 1752 they were ordered for all grenadiers.) A pipe-clayed match may have been worn at the back of the belt; the 24th Regiment (and perhaps others) wore their match-case in that position. Grenades were not carried at this time and both match-case and match were symbolic. This soldier wears his lapels buttoned half across, and his waistbelt with sword and bayonet over his coat. He wears an extra cartridge-box on a tan or buff strap buckled over his waistbelt. These were certainly adopted by grenadiers, and by line troops in Germany in 1763, and probably saw widespread use by infantry of all companies.

It was customary to combine the grenadier companies of regiments in the field to form a grenadier battalion: at Quebec the 'Louisbourg Grenadiers' led by Wolfe in person were made up of the grenadier companies of the 22nd, 40th and 45th Foot stationed at Louisbourg. Many officers deplored this practice, which tended to rob battalions of their best men, potential NCOs.

Contemporary illustrations sometimes show the uniforms as being fairly tight, and this was not only due to the influence of military fashion. The cloth was supposed to be 'pre-shrunk' before issue but often was not – until the first shower of rain. Each man had to make do with a single suit of clothes, and must often have shown many carefully hidden signs of hard wear and tear. Although waistcoats were worn for drill, and coarse smock-like shirts for rough work and fatigues (since 1749), the life of the soldier must have been one long round of mending and patching; in Germany the coat-sleeves of the band – who wore modified uniforms – were used for patching material. Inspection returns often mention worn-out equipment and 'bad clothing'.

A3: Private, Battalion Company, 43rd Regiment of Foot, marching order, 1750s This soldier wears brown marching gaiters with bone buttons, his neckcloth or 'roller' loosened, and he is heavily laden for the march.

A4: Sergeant, Battalion Company, 27th (Inniskilling) Regiment of Foot, 1750s Sergeants carried halberds, which by the 1750s were mere symbols of rank and of use only to push crooked ranks of men into position; there was no sharpened edge, and construction was too weak for the halberds to be useful as a weapon. On campaign in America they were usually left in store and a musket and bayonet substituted. The sergeant's badge of rank was a crimson sash with a narrow central line of facing colour, worn round the waist. This sergeant is further distinguished by silver lace on his hat and uniform. For parades and guard duty, all ranks wore white linen gaiters with black bone or horn buttons up the outside; 'join' ration beef bones provided an unending source for these.

PLATE B

B1: Private, Virginia Regiment, 1755 It seems that most, if not all, of the provincial troops with Braddock wore civilian dress or hunting shirts on campaign, including most of the officers.

B2: Petty Officer, Royal Navy, 1755 This tough sailor formed part of the contingent from HMS *Norwich* under Lieutenant Charles Spendlowe, RN. The seaman of the Royal Navy had no formal uniform at this time, but bulk purchase of clothing led to a certain uniformity. His small 'apple pie' cocked hat, blue jacket, black neckerchief and petticoat breeches and stockings are typical.

B3: Staff Officer, 1755 This officer, a member of Braddock's staff, wears a plain red frock over a gold-laced waistcoat. Many officers wore fairly plain or simply gold-laced red or blue coats on campaign. He wears his oldest and most comfortable riding breeches and boots. His horse has been shot from under him.

B4: Private, Battalion Company, 1755 The 48th Foot – later, 1st Battalion the Northamptonshire Regiment – wore buff facings and brass buttons. The regimental lace had a green and yellow stripe and a green scroll pattern.

General Braddock drew up detailed orders covering the dress and conduct of his troops on campaign, and his concern for detail shows that while he may have been one of the 'old school' he was certainly not stupid. His men were ordered to leave behind as much of their heavy kit as possible, and to discard their waist- and shoulder-belts and their swords. One must presume that they carried their cartridges, and perhaps their bayonet frogs, on waist-straps like those worn by the grenadiers. Sergeants retained their swords, but substituted muskets for halberds. Though the men were necessarily burdened with rations, spare shirts and shoes and so forth, the orders threatened dire punishment to any fool who used his musket as a convenient slinging-pole for equipment 'or by Any other means encumber his Firelock...' Because of the hot weather woollen breeches and waistcoats were replaced by small-clothes of 'Oznaburg', or coarse linen, which may have been brown, dyed red, or of natural colour. Thin pads or bladders of leather were placed in the hat between lining and crown as protection against the hot sun, a practice which was generally ordered for all troops in hot climates from 1761 onward. Brown canvas marching gaiters were issued.

A report on the exact equipment, and the weight of every buckle, garter and pouch carried by the British infantryman in 1762 survives; it was compiled by Lieutenant Alexander Baillie, 1st Battalion Royal American Regiment, for Colonel Henry Bouquet. The whole amounted to 65lb 12oz, including every stitch worn and every item carried in full marching order in America. Of this, actual clothing accounted for 13lb 8oz; belts, pouches, knapsack, haversack, and the contents thereof, 32lb (including six days' rations); and weapons and ammunition, 20lb 4oz.

B5: Private, Battalion Company, 44th Regiment of Foot, 1755 The private wears the 44th's yellow ochre facings and white lace, with a blue and black zigzag divided by a yellow stripe. His uniform has been adapted in the same way as the 48th's.

Officers would have worn boots, and almost certainly sashes and gorgets, their proud badges of rank. Company officers would have discarded their half-pikes or espontoons when in the forests, and most carried fusils in addition to their swords.

The regimental and king's colours of each battalion were carried by two ensigns, the most junior regimental officers. Often of very tender years, these lads must have found the six-foot-square colours difficult to handle in a high wind. The first or king's colour was the Union flag, with a wreath of roses and thistles placed centrally containing the regimental number. The Regimental Colour was of the facing colour, with the Union flag in the upper canton. The number appeared in the wreath of roses and thistles, except for those regiments granted special badges, or those with red or white as their facing colour; in the latter case the Second Colour was to comprise the Cross of St George with the Union flag in the upper canton.

PLATE C

C1: Soldier of the Independent Companies, 1755 Various Independent Companies were formed and sent on garrison duty to the colonies, and these units are known to have been stationed in the West Indies, Georgia and New York, among other places. There is little firm evidence of their uniforms in the 1750s. In the 1730s they were ordered to wear red coats faced and lined green; and those serving in the West Indies (then rather a vague term used to cover many overseas stations) were to have their coats lined with brown linen, which showed when the skirts were hooked back for ease of marching. Descriptions of deserters in 1755 mention coats of 'red turned with green'; and the wash drawing in the text shows officers with laced buttonholes. The number of companies in North America varied as new ones were raised and others transferred or re-formed. The constant changes must have led to great variations in uniform. A composite company served with Washington at Fort Necessity, and with Braddock in 1755. The surviving privates were transferred to the 50th Foot while the officers and NCOs went to South Carolina to recruit the companies back to strength.

C2: Private, the Virginia Regiment, 1755–62 Many militiamen fought in civilian clothes, and were offered cash bounties if they brought their own guns. Items of equipment, coats, hats, or complete uniforms were provided by some states, however. Massachusetts troops serving with William Johnson in 1755 wore blue coats faced red, a favourite colonial colour scheme also worn by troops from New Jersey, Pennsylvania and Virginia. Some Pennsylvanians also wore green coats faced red, and in 1757 New Yorkers wore 'dark drab turned up with middle drab cloth'. Red was also popular, and presumably the red cloth of regular army uniforms was readily available. Officers usually bought their own uniforms, and all were more or less based on the uniforms of the king's troops.

The Virginia Regiment was raised in 1754, and at first only the officers were uniformed. Later that year uniforms were issued, and there are various references to 'red coats and breeches', 'red coats faced blue' and 'thunder and lightning jackets (German serge) and red breeches'. Blue coats were also issued, and the Virginia companies with Braddock may well have worn a variety of uniforms, some with the coats cropped short. George Washington and other officers and men laid aside their regimentals and wore hunting shirt or soldier coats. When the regiment was reorganised late in 1755, the uniform was established as blue faced red; officers' uniforms were silver-laced, although they were ordered to have a suit of ordinary soldier's clothes for campaigning. This soldier carries a rifle with which he is about to demonstrate his skill, shooting at a board covered in white paper and marked with a black spot, as described for the 42nd in 1759.

C3: Typical campaign dress This consisted of a hunting shirt, which might be made of almost any material and vary in colour from natural linen, practical soft greys and browns through to showy red or almost white buckskin.

His cocked hat has its front two sides let down to shade his eyes, and his legs are protected against the woodland brush by woollen cloth leggings, of the style copied from the Indians and adopted eventually by much of the army.

Trousers were frequently worn; brown, linen and checked materials are mentioned, and buckskin breeches were very popular, particularly among Pennsylvanian 'German' settlers.

C4: Officer, New Jersey Blues They were raised in 1755 and won a reputation for discipline and good conduct. They were at Oswego and Ticonderoga and fought through until 1763. Their uniform was a short 'highland' jacket, blue-faced and cuffed red, with no lace, and blue breeches and white spatterdashes. A portrait of an officer shows a red, gold-laced waistcoat and blue breeches.

C5: Officers, 2nd Connecticut Regiment, 1758 The costume of the well-dressed officer is largely based upon a portrait of Colonel Nathan Whiting, who commanded a provincial battalion at Ticonderoga in 1758. He is dressed as for a parade. His regimentals are of fashionable cut, a scarlet coat with slashed cuffs of yellow, a yellow waistcoat with silver lace, and scarlet breeches. He wears the usual insignia of commissioned rank – a silver gorget suspended round his neck on a ribbon of facing colour, and a crimson silk net sash over the shoulder. He wears a liberally powdered wig of the popular contemporary style known as a 'pigeon-winged toupée'; the powder frosting his shoulders was quite acceptable socially, and appears in several contemporary portraits of gentlemen.

His companion is much more soberly (and less expensively) dressed. Red was a very popular colour among provincial officers and soldiers.

PLATE D

D1: Officer, Rogers' Rangers Many provincials came from long-settled communities, had seldom seen an Indian, and had less idea of what to do if ambushed than the average English regular. However, the Ranger companies were usually recruited from the frontier villages, although many of these were comparatively new immigrants. Though it is hard to say what proportion had previous military experience, they were certainly at home in the woods, and their natural independence and toughness enabled them to mature quickly under the spur of hard experience. With a nucleus of real frontiersmen, they soon became, when at their best, a first-class instrument for irregular warfare. They scouted far behind French 'lines', ambushed and raided, and were ambushed and raided in turn. Contemporary opinions of their effectiveness were mixed. Their unreliability and ill-discipline lost them the admiration and respect won by their frequent acts of daring.The most famous were Rogers' Rangers – originally the Ranger Company of Blanchard's New Hampshire Regiment – who were later expanded into His Majesty's Independent Companies of American Rangers. With a maximum strength of seven companies, they were neither regulars nor provincials, but were paid by the Crown. Rogers, however admirable a frontier fighter, was no angel, nor famous for his modesty and honesty. His 'journal', published in London after the war, began a long succession of works that exaggerated and glorified the role played by the Rangers.

Little is known of the officers' uniform beyond the fact that they may have worn green with silver lace. There seems to be no historical evidence to support the suggestion that the green-clad figure in West's painting *The Death of Wolfe* is a Rogers' Ranger, nor that the 'portrait' print based on it in any way resembles Rogers or his uniforms.

British infantry hairstyles: Left, Morier, 1760s. Note angle of fashionably cocked hat. Reconstruction of usual British private's hair, plaited and turned up under the hat, held in place with a comb. After Gilray, 1790s. Right, Three illustrations showing the side-locks, grown long and usually worn in two tight curls in front of the ears.

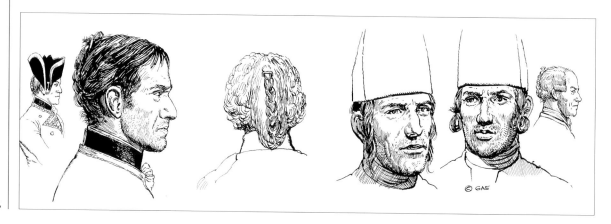

D2: Ranger, His Majesty's Independent Companies of American Rangers, 1758 Some attempt was made at a uniform dress, which varied within each company. Some, at least, of Rogers' men are known to have worn short green frieze jackets – made up by Messrs. Thos. and Benjamin Forseys of Albany – from 1758 onwards. The Scots bonnet was popular headgear, probably familiar to many of the men all their lives, and this costume seems to have caught the general fancy, '...those who can get them wear nothing else when they go out...' Buckskin breeches were worn, with leggings of green or brown rateen. Hunting smocks may have been the more usual dress when the Rangers 'went out'.

D3: Ranger, later 1750s In 1759 Captain John Knox of the 43rd Foot described Rangers wearing 'black rateen' – a coarse frieze cloth – lapelled and cuffed with blue; a sleeved waistcoat, a short jacket without sleeves, white metal buttons, canvas or linen 'drawers', and a short 'petticoat' or kilt made with a waistband and one button, open in front, black 'leggins' which buttoned on the calf, and Highland bonnets. The very Scots character of this costume seems to confirm the influence of traditional dress among Rangers recruited from recently settled Scots immigrants. It was very like the dress worn by common seamen or working men in certain parts of the British Isles.

D4: Rogers' Rangers, Stockbridge Indians Rogers recruited a company of Stockbridge Indians as scouts, but we know nothing of their clothing. These two wear typical hairstyles and a mixture of native and European dress.

D5: Rangers 1758–61 Although Rogers' attracted most of the publicity, then and since, there were other companies of Rangers serving with the British Army in America. Among them was Captain Hezekiah Dunn's Company of Rangers, raised in New Jersey. A deserter was described as wearing '...provincial clothing viz., a grey lapell'd waistcoat and an under green jacket, a leather cap, and Buckskin Breeches...' Each officer and man was furnished with a good blanket, underjacket, kersey lapelled jacket, buckskin breeches, shoes, stockings, leather cap and hatchet. Major Gorham's Company of Rangers in 1761 wore red coats with brown linings and facings (so that the coat could be reversed, brown faced red, in the field), brown waistcoats, and leather 'jockey' caps with an oakleaf or branch painted on the left side.

PLATE E

E1: Senior Officer, 1st or Royal Regiment of Foot, late 1750s All regiments bearing the 'Royal' title wore blue facings and blue breeches. This senior officer has the usual marks of rank, and his coat is richly laced with gold. He is booted and spurred for riding. In the winter of 1757-58 this unit (later, The Royal Scots) had nine companies at Albany and one company at Stillwater. The 2nd Battalion was at Quebec in 1759, and during the following winter the companies were dispersed once again: four to Amboy, New Jersey, four to Brunswick, and two to Trenton, New Jersey.

E2: Officer, Grenadier Company 46th Regiment of Foot This grenadier officer of 'Murray's Bucks', as this smart regiment was known, wears his uniform for a parade, with a richly embroidered mitre cap, and the regiment's gold lace on his facings. His hair is powdered and he wears his crimson sash over his shoulder, a gilt gorget suspended around his neck from a facing colour ribbon, and white gaiters. In the field he would normally have worn a cocked hat and boots.

E3: Infantry Officer in field dress, 1758 This officer has adapted to campaign conditions simply by wearing a plain red 'frock' – a less ornamented coat than his regimentals, without facings – and his hunting clothes from England. He has uncocked his hat – just as he might have done at home – and carries his sporting gun, powder flask and shot bag.

E4: Fifer, Drummer, 35th Foot, late 1750s Drummers and fifers of the Foot Guards and Royal Regiments wore the royal livery of red and blue. Line drummers wore coats of facing colour – in this case orange – with cuffs, lapels and linings of red, the whole profusely decorated with regimental pattern lace '...as the Colonel shall think fit'. The cap was decorated with a trophy of drums and banners; the back, formerly a hanging bag, seems sometimes to have been stiffened like a grenadier mitre cap at this period. Few regiments had extra musicians. Those there were, were not 'official' but were probably uniformed like the drummers.

In the noise and confusion of battle the drummers performed a very necessary duty by relaying the officers' commands in the form of different rhythms; and a long and weary march could be made to seem shorter if accompanied by the music of fifes and drums. Drummers were also used as messengers, and one of their other – less pleasant – duties was the infliction of punishment. It was the regimental drummers who wielded the cat when a flogging was ordered. Punishment in the British Army at that time was savage, and completely at the whim of the commanding officer. Some were sadists who ordered horrific numbers of lashes, while other regiments did very well with a minimum of floggings; the orderly book of the 44th Foot contains one passage of instructions to officers and NCOs on the treatment of men brought in drunk which is impressive for its enlightenment. Again, it must be remembered that this was a brutal age, both in civilian and military life, and that Wolfe's army certainly included many hair-raising 'hard cases' who felt that they had not proved their manhood until they had 'kissed the cat'.

The 35th later became 1st Battalion, Royal Sussex Regiment.

PLATE F

F1: Private, 80th Regiment of Light Armed Foot (Gage's Light Infantry), 1758 Recruited in the winter of 1757-58, this battalion, some 500 strong, did valuable service in America until 1764. It fought in some notable actions in the French and Indian War, and some elements particularly distinguished themselves at Detroit during Pontiac's Rebellion. The men seemed to have included a high proportion of independent-minded individualists better suited for the scouting, advance guard and rear guard duties of the light infantry than for line service.

The brown jacket without facings or lace was not a field-service modification, but the prescribed regimental dress, a fact confirmed by official documents. This short and practical combat garment was locally procured until 1763; in that year the unit changed to more conventional red regimentals faced orange. The buttons of the brown jacket were black. This soldier wears one of the many variations of the cap which originated in the cut-down cocked hat, and carries only the lightest equipment: shot bag and powder horn, cartridge-box on a waistbelt shortened, bayonet and hatchet. Many of the muskets carried by light troops were shortened, and some had browned barrels: 'carbines' were later issued, although the exact definition of a 'carbine' at this period is uncertain.

F2: Light Infantrymen, 1759 This man's clothing is the logical conclusion of the piecemeal measures adopted over a number of seasons of campaigning. The following description appears in Captain John Knox's *An Historical Journal of the Campaigns in North America for the years 1757, 1758, 1759 and 1760*, published by the Champlain Society in Toronto in 1914 and relevant to May 1759:

'The following order for the dress of the light infantry as approved by his Excellency Gen. Amherst: Maj. Gen. Wolfe desires the same may be exactly conformed to by the light troops under his command: the sleeves of the coat are put on the waistcoat, and instead of coat-sleeves, he has two wings like the grenadiers, but fuller; and a round slope reaching about half-way down his arm; which makes his coat of no incumbrance to him, but can be split off with pleasure; he has no lace, but the lapels remain; besides the usual pockets, he has two, not quite so high as his breast, made of leather, for ball and flints; and a flap of red cloth on the inside, which secures the ball from rolling out, if he should fall.

'His knapsack is carried very high between his shoulders, as the Indians carry their pack. His cartouch-box hangs under his arm on the left side, slung with a leathern strap; and his horn under the other arm on the right, hanging by a narrower web than that used by his knapsack; his canteen down his back, under his knapsack, and covered with cloth; he has a rough case for his tomahock, with a button; and it hangs in a leathern sling down his side, like a hanger, between his coat and waistcoat. No bayonet (Gen. Wolfe ordered the light infantry to wear their bayonets); his leggings have leathern straps under his shoes, like spatterdashes; his hat is made into a cap, with a flap and button, and with as much black cloth added as will come under his chin, and keep him warm, when he lies down; it hooks in the front, and is made like the old velvet caps in England.'

F3: Officer, 40th Foot, 1758–59 The popular myth of the wars in America, to the effect that all American troops were expert woods fighters and all British troops were blundering ignoramuses, has been wildly exaggerated. Many British officers were hardened professionals, accustomed since childhood to country life, hunting, and the handling of firearms. By 1759 the harsh first-hand experience of the French and Indian War had brought to many of them a familiar skill in forest fighting and woodcraft. Men like Wolfe and Lord Howe appreciated the need for practical dress and tactics, and were energetic reformers. Some of the more self-consciously elegant officers were certainly mildly appalled at the orders to crop their hair, wear cut-down soldiers' uniforms, and do their own cooking and laundry, but there is no doubt that they obeyed.

This officer has removed all lace from his shortened coat, and wears a soldier's waistcoat. He retains his sash; some retained both sash and gorget, some discarded both. He carries a fusil with shortened bayonet, a 'belly box' for cartridges and a powder horn, and carries a hatchet instead of a sword. The leather 'jockey' cap was already in use by some

horsemen and sportsmen in England and, as other figures on these pages show, was often improvised by cutting down a cocked hat.

F4: Grenadier, 60th (Royal American) Regiment of Foot, 1759 The 60th, ancestor of the King's Royal Rifle Corps, was raised during the course of the war (25 December 1755) from local recruits. Four battalions were recruited in Massachusetts, New York, Pennsylvania, Maryland and North Carolina, and were later augmented by volunteers from England. Many of the officers were European professionals with local commissions, and the first two battalion commanders were Swiss. Many of the men were of German and Swiss immigrant stock. The emphasis in training and use of this unit was upon forest fighting, and drill and disciplinary requirements were to some extent relaxed. (The original title – 62nd Royal American Regiment – was changed to that quoted in 1757.)

No picture of the uniform of other ranks of the 60th survives from earlier than 1768. For this reconstruction we have presumed that grenadiers followed the dress of line troops closely, and this figure illustrates several innovations typical of the early 1760s. Military fashion usually precedes the regulations, and it became the practice to cover the mitre cap with fur before this style was officially authorised. The 60th wore the red-faced-blue of all Royal regiments, without lace; this coat is cut fairly short. The waistbelt and bayonet frog, with a hatchet replacing the sword, are worn over the shoulder – an increasingly popular fashion which eventually led to the wearing of the bayonet on a 'purpose-built' shoulder-belt. The black gaiters have leather tops cut away at the back, and to protect the knees of the breeches from the leather, white canvas knee-cuffs are worn, as was the practice in the cavalry. The heart decorations at the tips of the hooked-up coat skirts are typical of the period.

F5: Soldiers, 55th Foot, 1758 The 55th Foot (later 1st Battalion, the Border Regiment) was Lord Howe's regiment, and these soldiers display the field modifications introduced by that energetic and gifted commander for the Ticonderoga campaign of 1758. (The 55th are listed as having green facings and yellow lace in 1761, but absolute confirmation of their distinctions in 1758 is lacking.)

The severely cropped cocked hats have a brim only two-and-a-half inches wide, worn slouched; the green sprigs are worn in celebration of the king's birthday. Eyewitnesses of the day describe how the coats were docked short so as not to encumber the men in thick forest. For ease and comfort, the hair was cropped, and in this, as in every other measure, Lord Howe set a personal example. Hatchets are carried instead of a sword, and an extra cartridge-box at the waist brings the total ammunition carried by each man up to 36 rounds. Many of the muskets were shortened, and the ten best marksmen in each battalion were issued with 'rifled barrelled guns' probably of German jäger pattern. Each man carried in his knapsack a large supply of meal, which he was expected to cook for himself; and when on the march the bare necessities were carried rolled up in a blanket.

PLATE G

G1: Officer, Royal Artillery, 1759 At this period two guns – light three- and six-pounders – were generally attached to each infantry battalion, with a detachment of an officer, two NCOs and 12 men. The Royal Artillery was noted for the rapidity and accuracy of its fire, and for the cleanliness and good quality of its equipment. This senior officer wears the traditional blue uniform faced red with gold lacing. From 1758, the yellow lace which previously decorated the waistcoats of other ranks was discontinued. Sergeants wore two gold-lace shoulder-knots, corporals two worsted knots, and bombardiers one. This officer follows normal practice in wearing the soft-topped 'jockey' boots popular at this period; other ranks wore black cloth gaiters on all occasions except full-dress parades, when white ones were substituted. The other ranks carried haversacks and knapsacks, and flintlock muskets; there is some evidence that NCOs were armed with the shorter fusils or carbines during the 1750s. Officers usually carried fusils in the field, although this practice declined during the 1760s.

G2: Captain of over three years' seniority, Royal Navy The Royal Navy gave invaluable assistance during the landings in Canada, and James Cook, the famous navigator, drew magnificent charts of the St Lawrence. Naval officers and seamen not only manned landing-barges during amphibious operations but also frequently served guns ashore since there was much block-and-tackle work to be done.

Officers of the Royal Navy first received a uniform in 1748. Junior captains had blue lapels, commanders had blue lapels and blue cuffs, and lieutenants had plain blue without lace. The midshipman's white collar patch appeared in 1758. Close co-operation between the Army and the Royal Navy was essential during the campaign against Quebec.

G3: Major-General James Wolfe, 1759 As far as can be ascertained there was no regulation dress for general officers at this period; portraits usually show them wearing scarlet and blue laced with gold, and the spacing of the laced buttonholes may have indicated exact rank. Plainer dress was usually worn in the field. A sketch of Wolfe, made at Quebec by or for one of his ADCs, Captain Harvey Smyth, has survived and less flattering caricatures by Townshend show him in what was obviously his preferred field dress. The young general is shown wearing a severely practical red coat and waistcoat and blue breeches. He wears what are perhaps gaiters with leather tops; the buttons are visible in the original sketch, and they cover the knee. In an age when generals were not infrequently killed in action, it is understandable that Wolfe carried a fusil and wore a cartridge-box and bayonet on a waistbelt – all these features are shown plainly in the sketch from life. The black armband was worn in mourning for his father who had died recently; all officers of the army wore such bands in April 1759 in mourning for the Princess of Orange. Officers' hair was usually unpowdered on service, and sometimes cropped, either as a conscious 'front-line' precaution or because the individual normally wore a wig.

G4: Private, Battalion Company, 78th Foot (Fraser's Highlanders), 1757-63 This short-lived unit was raised in 1757 by the Hon. Simon Fraser, and fought at Louisbourg and the Plains of Abraham. Little is known about the uniform; it would have been similar to that worn by the Black Watch, with light buff facings. It is not known for certain whether the dark 'Government sett' tartan of the Black Watch was worn. In bad weather the plaid was often worn over the head and used to muffle the musket as well. The plaid consisted of 12 yards of cloth folded in pleats, belted round the waist to form a kilt with the remainder pinned up to the shoulder.

The short red Highland jacket is worn over a red waistcoat, which latter was the normal hot weather working and field dress. The dark blue bonnet has a black cockade sewn on; the sporran or goatskin purse is of the plainest design at this period. Breeches of coarse linen and infantry gaiters or cloth leggings were often worn in place of the kilt for working details, and hose and separate socks may have been worn, like the 42nd Regiment. All leather is black; the cartridge-box bears the royal cipher, and is worn with the bayonet frog, on the waistbelt. A broadsword is carried on a shoulder-belt. The 42nd Regiment wore the same uniform, cuffed and collared blue and with white lace with two red stripes. Officers wore gold lace.

PLATE H

H1: Sergeant, 58th Regiment of Foot, winter dress, late 1750s This soldier wears a common North American winter garment, the Canadian capote, with his equipment belted over it; under it his red coat faced black. British soldiers were not issued overcoats, although a small number of 'watch coats' were issued to each battalion for the use of sentries; so it is certain that thick winter coats must have been improvised for wear in the very severe American winter. This sergeant's sash, red with a black strip is tied over his equipment.

H2: Grenadier, 28th Regiment, winter dress This soldier wears his uniform coat buttoned over a second coat and thick woollen stockings pulled over his gaiters and shoes. 'Ice-creepers' are strapped on his feet to prevent a fall on the frozen ground.

H3: Private, 17th Regiment, winter dress, 1759 Forage caps for the soldiers were made from left-overs from converted coats, and usually seem to have taken the form of red stocking caps with small turned-up flaps of facing colour marked with the regimental number. Items like this, made up within the regiment were rarely uniform and may have varied from company to company. Some of the British garrison of newly-captured Quebec were given French uniform coats and 'moggosans' as part of their winter clothing; and he wears his over his own red coat.

H4: Officers and men in winter dress The officer has a green civilian greatcoat with large collar buttoned around his chin. The ensign shivers in a blue frock.

Hard campaigning, deteriorating uniforms and improvised cold weather gear gave the ragged, bearded British regulars the appearance of Hungarian or Croatian irregulars 'droll and grotesque, more like a sand digger or hod-carrier than a soldier'.

Notes sur les planches en couleur

A1 Caporal, Compagnie de bataillon, 45e à pied, vers 1750. Les caporaux se distinguaient par un nœud de ruban blanc sur l'épaule droite. Ce détail mis à part, il s'agit de l'uniforme de base de l'ensemble du bataillon des hommes 'de chapeau'. **A2** Grenadier, 15e à pied (Amherst) en Amérique, 1758-67. Les grenadiers se distinguaient par leur haut calot en mitre, leurs boîtes d'allumettes et leurs 'ailettes' (décorations aux épaules). **A3** Simple soldat, Compagnie de bataillon, 43e régiment à pied, ordre de marche, vers 1750 lourdement chargés pour la marche. **A4** Sergent, Compagnie de bataillon, 27e Régiment à pied (Inniskilling), vers 1750. Les sergents portaient une hallebarde, qui était devenue vers 1750 un simple symbole de rang et qu'ils utilisaient uniquement pour forcer les rangs d'hommes tordus à se remettre en place.

B1 Simple soldat, Régiment de Virginie, 1755. Il semble que la plupart, sinon la totalité des troupes provinciales de Braddock étaient habillées en civil ou en chemise de chasse en campagne, y compris les officiers. **B2** Second maître, Royal Navy, 1755. Ce marin est uniforme typique faisait partie du contingent du HMS Norwich. **B3** Officier d'État-Major, 1755, qui porte une veste rouge simple sur un gilet brodé d'or. Il porte sa culotte de cheval en daim la plus vieille et la plus confortable, et les bottes. **B4** Simple soldat, Compagnie de bataillon, 1755. Durant les campagnes, on ordonnait aux hommes d'abandonner autant que possible leur paque-tage lourd. **B5** Simple soldat, Compagnie de bataillon, 44e Régiment à pied, 1755. Ce simple soldat porte les parements jaune ocre du 44e et le galon blanc, avec les zigzags bleus et noirs divisés par une bande jaune.

C1 Soldat des Compagnies Indépendantes, 1755. Diverses Compagnies Indépendantes furent formées et envoyées aux colonies, mais on sait très peu de choses certaines sur leurs uniformes. **C2** Simple soldat, Régiment de Virginie, 1755-62. Diverses milices combattirent parmi les provinciaux et recevaient une prime s'ils apportaient leur propre fusil. **C3** L'uniforme de campagne typique était composé d'une chemise de chasse, qui pouvait être réalisée en n'importe quel tissu, et dont la couleur variait. **C4** Officier, New Jersey Blues. Ils furent levés en 1755 et firent une réputation de discipline et de bonne conduite. **C5** Officiers, 2e Régiment du Connecticut, 1758. Cet officier bien habillé est habillé comme pour un défilé. Son compagnon est bien plus sobrement habillé (et moins coûteusement).

D1 Officier, Rangers de Rogers. Avec un groupe de vrais pionniers, ces hommes devinrent vite, quand ils donnaient le meilleur d'eux-mêmes, un instrument de première classe de guerre irrégulière. **D2** Ranger, Compagnies Indépendantes de Rangers Américains de Sa Majesté, 1758. On remarque quelques tentatives dans la direction d'un uniforme, qui variait au sein de chaque compagnie. **D3** Ranger, après 1755. Le caractère très écossais de ce costume semble confirmer l'influence des costumes traditionnels parmi les Rangers recrutés parmi les immigrants écossais récemment installés. **D4** Rangers de Rogers, Indiens de Stockbridge. Rogers recruta une compagnie d'Indiens de Stockbridge comme éclaireurs, mais nous ne connaissons rien de leur uniforme. **D5** Rangers 1758-61. Bien que les Rangers de Rogers s'attirèrent la plus grande publicité, il y avait d'autres compagnies de Rangers qui servaient avec l'armée britannique en Amérique.

E1 Officier supérieur, 1er Régiment (ou Royal) à Pied, après 1755, avec toutes les marques de rang habituelles. Tous les régiments qui portaient le titre de 'Royal' portaient des parements et une culotte bleus. **E2** Officier, Compagnie de Grenadiers, 46e Régiment à pied. Cet officier des grenadiers de 'Murray's Bucks', le nom sous lequel on connaissait ce régiment élégant, porte un uniforme de parade. **E3** Officier d'infanterie en uniforme de campagne, 1758. Cet officier s'est adapté aux conditions de campagne en portant simplement une 'veste' rouge simple et ses vêtements de chasse apportés d'Angleterre. **E4** Fifre, Tambour, 35e à pied, après 1755, qui porte la livrée royale de rouge et bleu. Les tambours étaient également utilisés comme messagers, et l'une de leurs autres responsabilités (moins agréables) était d'infliger les châtiments.

F1 Simple soldat, 80e Régiment de Fantassins légers (Infanterie Légère de Gage), 1758. Parmi ces hommes, il semblerait y avoir eu une grande proportion d'individualistes de nature indépendante, mieux adaptés aux responsabilités d'éclaireurs, de garde avancée et d'arrière-garde dans l'infanterie légère qu'à celles du service sur le front. **F2** Soldats d'infanterie légère, 1759. Les vêtements de cet homme représentent la conclusion logique des mesures fragmentaires adoptées durant plusieurs saisons de campagne. **F3** Officier, 40e à pied, 1758-59. De nombreux officiers britanniques étaient des professionnels endurcis, habitués depuis l'enfance à la vie à la campagne, la chasse et la manipulation des armes à feu. Ils comprenaient la néces-sité d'avoir un uniforme et des tactiques pratiques. **F4** Grenadier, 60e Régiment (Américain Royal) à pied, 1759. Beaucoup d'hommes faisaient partie des immigrants allemands et suisses. L'entraînement et l'utilisation de cette unité se concentraient sur les combats en forêt. Les exigences en matière d'exercices et de discipline étaient quelque peu relaxées. **F5** Soldats, 55e à pied, 1758. Le 55e à pied était le régiment de Lord Howe, et ces soldats présen-tent les modifications de terrain qu'il introduisit pour la campagne de Ticonderoga en 1758.

G1 Officier, Artillerie Royale, 1759. L'Artillerie Royale était notée pour la rapidité et la précision de son feu, et pour la propreté et la bonne qualité de son matériel. **G2** Capitaine de plus de trois ans d'ancienneté, Royal Navy. Les officiers navals et les marins s'occupaient non seulement des chalands de débarquement durant les opérations amphibie, mais servaient souvent les canons à terre. **G3** Major-Général James Wolfe, 1759. Il semblerait qu'à cette période il n'existait pas d'uniforme réglementaire pour les officiers généraux. Il porte un brassard noir en signe de deuil pour son père, récemment décédé. **G4** Simple soldat, compagnie de bataillon, 78e à Pied (Highlanders de Fraser), 1757-63. On connaît peu de choses sur l'uniforme du 78e. Il était sans doute similaire à celui du Black Watch, avec des parements chamois-clair.

H1 Sergent, 58e Régiment à pied, uniforme d'hiver, après 1750, qui porte la capote canadienne, avec son équipement par-dessus. En dessous, il porte son manteau rouge aux parements noirs. **H2** Grenadier, 28e Régiment, uniforme d'hiver. Ce soldat porte son manteau d'uniforme boutonné sur un second manteau et des bas de laine épais par-dessus ses guêtres et ses chaussures. Il a attaché des 'ice creepers' à ses pieds pour lui éviter de tomber sur la glace. **H3** Simple soldat, 17e Régiment, uniforme d'hiver, 1759. Les shakos étaient confectionnés avec les restes des manteaux ajustés. Les articles tels que ceux-ci, confectionnés au sein du Régiment, étaient rarement uniformes et pouvaient varier d'une compagnie à l'autre. **H4** Officiers et hommes en uniforme d'hiver. Les dures campagnes, la détérioration de leurs uniformes et les vêtements improvisés pour se défendre du froid donnaient aux réguliers britanniques en haillons et barbus l'apparence d'irréguliers hongrois ou croates.

Farbtafeln

A1 Obergefreiter, Battalion Company, 45th Foot, 50er Jahre des 18. Jahrhunderts. Die Obergefreiten waren durch ein verschlungenes weißes Band auf der rechten Schulter erkenntlich. Ansonsten ist dies die Grunduniform aller Bataillone beziehungsweise der "Behüteten". **A2** Grenadier, 15th Foot (Amherst's), in Amerika, 1758-67. Die Grenadiere zeichneten sich durch ihre hohen "Bischofsmützen", den Tornister und Schulterabzeichen aus. **A3** Gefreiter, Battalion Company, 43rd Regiment of Foot, Marschordnung, 50er Jahre des 18. Jahrhunderts, schwer beladen auf dem Marsch. **A4** Feldwebel, Battalion Company, 27th (Inniskilling) Regiment of Foot, 50er Jahre des 18. Jahrhunderts. Die Feldwebel hatten Hellebarden bei sich, die jedoch in den 50er Jahren des 18. Jahrhunderts bereits lediglich als Zeichen des Ranges dienten und nur dazu verwendet wurden, die Soldaten in gerade Reihen zu drängen.

B1 Gefreiter, Virginia Regiment, 1755. Es hat den Anschein, als ob die meisten - wenn nicht alle - Truppen in der Provinz bei Braddock zivile Kleidung oder Jagdhemden trugen, selbst die Offiziere. **B2** Obermaat, Royal Navy, 1755. Dieser Matrose in der typischen Uniform gehörte zum Kontingent vom Schiff HMS Norwich. **B3** Stabsoffizier, 1755, in einem einfachen, roten Kittel über einer Weste mit Goldtressen. Er trägt seine ältesten und bequemsten Rehleder und Stiefel. **B4** Gefreiter, Battalion Company, 1755. Auf Feldzügen erhielten die Soldaten den Befehl, so viel wie möglich von ihrer schweren Ausrüstung zurückzulassen. **B5** Gefreiter, Battalion Company, 44th Regiment of Foot, 1755. Der Gefreite trägt die gelb-ocker-farbenen Aufschläge der 44th und weiße Litze mit einer blau-schwarzen Zickzacklinie, die von einem gelben Streifen unterbrochen wird.

C1 Soldat der Independent Companies, 1755. Es wurden mehrere Independent Companies aufgestellt und in die Kolonien entsandt, doch gibt es kaum zuverlässige Unterlagen hinsichtlich ihrer Uniformen. **C2** Gefreiter, Virginia Regiment, 1755-62. Zahlreiche Milizionäre kämpften in Zivilkleidung. Wenn sie ihr eigenes Gewehr mitbrachten, erhielten sie eine Geldsumme. **C3** Die typische Feldkleidung bestand aus einem Jagdhemd, das praktisch aus jedem Stoff sein konnte und verschiedene Farben aufwies. **C4** Offizier, New Jersey Blues. Diese Kompanie wurde 1755 aufgestellt und machte sich einen Namen für gute Disziplin und anständiges Betragen. **C5** Offiziere, 2nd Connecticut Regiment, 1758. Der gut gekleidete Offizier ist wie für eine Parade angezogen. Sein Kamerad weist eine viel schlichtere (und weniger kostspielige) Aufmachung auf.

D1 Offizier, Rogers' Rangers. Mit einem Kern aus echten Grenzbewohnern wurden diese Männer - wenn in Höchstform - schon bald zu einem erstklassigen Instrument der ungeregelten Kriegsführung. **D2** Ranger, His Majesty's Independent Companies of American Rangers, 1758. Zwar bemühte man sich um eine einheitliche Kleidung, doch unterschied sich die Aufmachung von Kompanie zu Kompanie. **D3** Ranger, Ende der 50er Jahre des 18. Jahrhunderts. Die deutlich schottische Prägung der Kleidung scheint den Einfluß der traditionellen Tracht unter den Rangers zu belegen, die aus den Reihen frisch angesiedelter schottischer Einwanderer rekrutiert wurden. **D4** Rogers' Rangers, Stockbridge-Indianer. Rogers warb eine Kompanie von Stockbridge-Indianern als Späher an, doch ist über deren Kleidung nichts bekannt. **D5** Rangers, 1758-61. Obgleich Rogers' damals wie heute den Großteil der Publicity auf sich zogen, gab es dennoch andere Kompanien von Rangers, die bei der britischen Armee in Amerika dienten.

E1 Dienstälterer Offizier, 1st bzw. Royal Regiment of Foot, Ende der 50er Jahre des 18. Jahrhunderts, mit den üblichen Rangabzeichen. Alle Regimenter, die den Namen "Royal" trugen, hatten blaue Uniformaufschläge und blaue Breeches. **E2** Offizier, Grenadier Company 46th Regiment of Foot. Dieser Grenadieroffizier von "Murray's Bucks", wie dieses schneidige Regiment genannt wurde, trägt seine Paradeuniform. **E3** Infanterieoffizier im Feldzug, 1758. Dieser Offizier hat sich den Bedingungen im Feld angepaßt, indem er einfach einen schlichten, roten "Kittel" und seine Jagdkleidung aus England trägt. **E4** Pfeifer, Trommler, 35th Foot, Ende der 50er Jahre des 18. Jahrhunderts, in der rot-blauen königlichen Livree. Die Trommler wurden auch als Boten eingesetzt, und eine ihrer - weniger angenehmen - Aufgaben bestand darin, Bestrafungen auszuteilen.

F1 Gefreiter, 80th Regiment of Light Armed Foot (Gage's Light Infantry), 1758. Unter den Männern scheint sich ein beträchtlicher Anteil von Individualisten mit unabhängiger Gesinnung befunden zu haben, die sich besser für die Aufklärung, die Vor- und Nachhut der leichten Infanterie eigneten als für den Dienst an der Front. **F2** Soldaten der leichten Infanterie, 1759. Die Kleidung dieses Soldaten stellt den logischen Schluß der stückweisen Maßnahmen dar, die im Verlauf mehrerer Perioden im Feld getroffen wurden. **F3** Offizier, 40th Foot, 1758-59. Unter den britischen Offizieren befanden sich zahlreiche abgehärtete Berufssoldaten, die von Kindesbeinen an das Landleben, die Jagd und die Handhabung von Waffen gewöhnt waren und sich der Notwendigkeit für praktische Uniform und Taktik bewußt waren. **F4** Grenadier, 60th (Royal American) Regiment of Fuß, 1759. Viele der Männer stammten von deutschen und schweizerischen Einwanderern ab. Bei der Ausbildung und dem Einsatz dieser Einheit lag der Schwerpunkt auf dem Waldkampf, und das Exerzieren sowie die Disziplin waren in gewissem Maß zweite Hand. **F5** Soldaten, 55th Foot, 1758. Das 55th Foot war Lord Howes Regiment, und diese Soldaten zeigen die Modifikationen im Feld, die er anläßlich des Ticonderoga-Feldzugs 1758 veranlaßte.

G1 Offizier, Royal Artillery, 1759. Die Royal Artillery war für die Schnelligkeit und die Treffsicherheit ihres Geschützfeuers sowie die Sauberkeit und hochwertige Qualität ihrer Ausrüstung bekannt. **G2** Korvettenkapitän mit über dreijähriger Dienstzeit, Royal Navy. Marineoffiziere und Matrosen stellten nicht nur die Besatzung für Landefahrzeuge bei Einsätzen zu Land und Wasser, sondern bedienten häufig auch Gewehre an Land. **G3** Generalmajor James Wolfe, 1759. Für Generaloffiziere scheint es in dieser Zeit keine vorschriftsmäßige Kleidung gegeben zu haben. Die schwarze Armbinde ist ein Zeichen der Trauer für seinen kürzlich verstorbenen Vater. **G4** Gefreiter, Battalion Company, 78th Foot (Fraser's Highlanders), 1757-63. Über die Uniform der 78th Foot ist nur wenig bekannt. Sie glich wahrscheinlich der der Black Watch, die hellgelbbraune Aufschläge hatte.

H1 Feldwebel, 58th Regiment of Foot, Winterkleidung, Ende der 50er Jahre des 18. Jahrhunderts. Der Soldat trägt den kanadischen Regenmantel mit seiner Koppel darüber; darunter seine rote Jacke mit schwarzen Aufschlägen. **H2** Grenadier, 28th Regiment, Winterkleidung. Dieser Soldat trägt seine Uniformjacke zugeknöpft über einer zweiten Jacke, dicke Wollstrümpfe über seinen Gamaschen und Schuhen. An seine Füße sind "Eisschuhe" geschnallt, um ein Ausrutschen auf dem Eis zu vermeiden. **H3** Gefreiter, 17th Regiment, Winterkleidung, 1759. Die Feldmützen waren aus Stoff, deren Umschneidern von Jacken übrig blieb. Kleidungsstücke wie diese, die innerhalb des Regiments gefertigt wurden, waren selten einheitlich und unterschieden sich unter Umständen von Kompanie zu Kompanie. **H4** Offiziere und Mannschaften in Winterkleidung. Anstrengende Feldzüge, verschlissene Uniformen und improvisierte Kleidungsstücke zum Schutz vor dem kalten Wetter ließen die zerzausten, bärtigen, regulären britischen Soldaten eher wie ungarische oder kroatische irreguläre Soldaten aussehen.